CITYSPOTS
DUBROVNIK

Helena Zukowski

D1325052

Written by Helena Zukowski
Original photography by Helena Zukowski
Front cover photography Keren Su/Getty Images
Series design based on an original concept by Studio 183 Limited

Produced by Cambridge Publishing Management Limited
Project Editor: Penny Isaac
Layout: Julie Crane
Maps: PC Graphics
Transport map: © Communicarta Limited

Published by Thomas Cook Publishing
A division of Thomas Cook Tour Operations Limited
Company Registration No. 1450464 England
PO Box 227, Unit 18, Coningsby Road
Peterborough PE3 8SB, United Kingdom
email: books@thomascook.com
www.thomascookpublishing.com
+44 (0)1733 416477
ISBN-13: 978-1-84157-729-6
ISBN-10: 1-84157-729-4

First edition © 2006 Thomas Cook Publishing
Text © 2006 Thomas Cook Publishing
Maps © 2006 Thomas Cook Publishing
Series Editor/Project Editor: Kelly Anne Pipes
Production/DTP: Steven Collins

Printed and bound in Spain by GraphyCems

CONTENTS

CITYSPOTS

SYMBOLS & ABBREVIATIONS
The following symbols are used throughout this book:

ⓐ address ⓣ telephone ⓕ fax ⓔ email ⓦ website address
ⓛ opening times ⓝ public transport connections ⓘ important

The following symbols are used on the maps:

🄸 information office	○ city
✈ airport	○ large town
✚ hospital	○ small town
🛡 police station	═ motorway
🚌 bus station	▬ main road
🚋 railway station	▬ minor road
✝ cathedral	▬ railway
❶ numbers denote featured cafés & restaurants	

Hotels and restaurants are graded by approximate price as follows:
£ budget ££ mid-range £££ expensive

▶ *The red roofs of Dubrovnik*

Introduction

So many words of praise have been heaped on Dubrovnik, which is known as the 'pearl of the Adriatic', that it has always shone like a beacon in the world of tourism. As part of the former Yugoslavia, it was an enormously popular sun-and-sea destination; no one was prepared for the economic problems that resulted from plummeting tourism during the Balkan wars. Over the past decade, however, the word that Croatia is back in business has been spreading like honey on a hot summer's day. Thanks to the welcoming nature of the Croatians, and a programme of studiously authentic rebuilding, the charm of Dubrovnik has reasserted itself and visitors can experience this captivating culture once again.

Part of the city's eternal allure may be the questions and contradictions that cling to it. How, for example, did Dubrovnik manage to hang on to its majestic city walls in the 19th century when every other city in Europe was tearing theirs down? How do the waters that lap Croatia's rugged coastline remain so incredibly clear and full of fish? How can a country that celebrates religious festivals with such fervour also be Europe's top naturist destination? And how has Dubrovnik managed to remain intact after so many centuries of invasion?

Like Prague, Dubrovnik always kept an eye on the future: when invaders flocked in and threatened to wreak havoc in the city, the citizens paid the conquerors to leave them alone. These invaders, who came from cities such as Venice, Istanbul, Budapest and Vienna, sometimes stayed and put down roots, leaving their imprint on the culture. It's no wonder that the citizens developed a great yearning to be part of the Western world. Now, as part of independent Croatia, the citizens of Dubrovnik feel sure that they will blend seamlessly in when the country joins the European Union in the near future.

Before the 1991–2 war, Croatia had long been home to minority populations, but in the 2001 census more than 90 per cent of the population identified itself as ethnically Croat. Croats warmly welcome visitors, and are committed to putting the horrors of the war and ethnic tensions behind them. The painstakingly restored Dubrovnik is, once again, in the words of George Bernard Shaw, a 'paradise on earth'.

◆ *Tourists have now returned to this beautiful city*

When to go

The ideal times to visit Dubrovnik are usually May, or the late summer and early autumn months. By then the major tourist push is over, yet the sea will still be warm and the days pleasantly balmy. Average temperatures in May are 23°C (73°F); in September the average is 27°C (80°F) and in October 22°C (72°F). For those interested in lots of activity and enjoying the limited range of nightlife, August is the best month to go, but it can be very hot and crowded then.

SEASONS & CLIMATE

On the Adriatic coast, Dubrovnik enjoys a Mediterranean climate with hot, dry summers and mild spring and autumn weather. Winter is generally cool and humid with a bite in the air.

The tourist season generally runs from April to October, with spring and summer the best time to enjoy activity holidays, including biking or hiking. The sea is usually warm for swimming between mid-May and early October.

SAINT BLAISE: THE PATRON SAINT OF DUBROVNIK

If you feel that eyes are watching you as you walk around Dubrovnik, it's likely to be those of Sveti Vlaho (St Blaise), whose image seems to be everywhere. He is the symbol of the Dubrovnik Republic and appears on the state flag and coins, on the cannons that were once placed along the city walls and over gateways into the city. Historically, St Blaise was a 4th-century physician and spiritual leader who, according to legend, saved the life of a child who was choking to death on a fish bone. He thus became the patron saint for people with ailments, particularly sore throats.

While a bishop, in AD 316, St Blaise became caught up in a sporadic anti-Christian campaign that was being waged by the Roman emperor Diocletian (even though the Edict of Milan, passed three years earlier, was supposed to allow Christians the freedom to practice their religion officially). No one is quite sure how he was martyred, but one account claims he was flayed to death with iron combs, which is why a comb is often used as his emblem; he is also the patron saint of wool-combers.

Four centuries after his death, a cathedral priest dreamt that St Blaise had appeared to him, telling him that a fleet of Venetian galleons were anchored off the island of Lokrum near Dubrovnik and pretending to take on water barrels, in reality they were preparing to attack. The priest warned the officials, saved the city, and St Blaise was officially made Dubrovnik's patron saint in 972. More recently, during the 1991 war, a group of Dubrovnik refugees, together with the Croatian president Stipe Mesić, invoked the aid of St Blaise before challenging the Montenegrin army and Yugoslavian navy. The publicity was such that the troops chose to leave rather than be accused of destroying one of the world's most beautiful walled cities. St Blaise is celebrated annually on 3 February with holy services and a parade of his relics around the town.

ANNUAL EVENTS

February

The Feast of St Blaise, on the 3rd of the month, celebrates the patron saint of Dubrovnik with a ceremonial holy service in front of the cathedral at 10.00 followed by a religious procession around town at 11.30 with the relics of St Blaise.

March/April

The Procession of the Religious Brotherhoods, in Korčula, is held on Good Friday.

May

The Moreška, on Korčula Island, is a traditional sword dance and drama that was popular throughout the Mediterranean at one time. It is now a major tourist attraction, and is officially staged on 29 July, which is the saint's day of St Theodore, the patron saint of Korčula. In fact, it has become a weekly summer event that starts in May and is staged every Thursday night until September. It commemorates the clash between Christians and Moors, when the Christians attempted to free a young girl kidnapped by the 'infidels'.

Feast of St Domnius is celebrated in Split on 7 May, with masses, processions and general festivities.

July

Of all the cultural festivals, the **Dubrovnik Summer Festival** from mid-July to mid-Aug is the most important. Founded in 1950, this highly acclaimed international festival hosts everything from ballet to Shakespeare, and performances take place in the squares and courtyards of the Old Town. Ⓦ www.dubrovnik-festival.hr

The Dalmatian Klapa Festival takes place in July near Split and seems to be gathering momentum, especially among younger people. Klapa is folk singing in vocal harmonies that are only rarely accompanied by instruments. Ⓦ www.klapa-trogir.com/klapas.htm
Split Jazz Festival held in early July.

August
Held in mid-August in Split, the **Festival of Creative Disorder** caters to more sub-cultural tastes, with various counter-cultural events and happenings.
Quarantine (Karantena), from late August to early September, is an international multimedia festival that features evening performances of contemporary theatre, music, film and dance, including alternative theatre and performance art.
Ⓦ www.karantena.mi2.hr

September
Staged in late September and early October, the **Festival of New Film and Video** in Split features independent short films from Croatia and full-length foreign releases.

November
All Saints Day, on 1 November, is when families visit the graves of deceased relatives.

⬤ *St Blaise: Dubrovnik's patron saint*

Dubrovnik Summer Festival

The Dubrovnik Summer Festival is the main event: Dubrovnik's most important cultural festival of the year bar none. Attracting an international line-up of artists, it's the biggest and best festival, not only in Dubrovnik, but in all of Croatia. Over the years, it has attracted such celebrated names as Herbert von Karajan, Yehudi

● *The summer festival showcases numerous musical and theatrical events*

Menuhin, Zubin Mehta, Monserrat Caballe, Isaac Stern and the Vienna Boys Choir. Don't expect to see The Red Hot Chili Peppers or Björk – the Dubrovnik Summer Festival celebrates ballet, opera, and jazz (stars like Duke Ellington and Dizzy Gillespie have played here).

The festival was born in September 1950 during a period when many theatrical and musical events were springing up all over Europe. Kicking off in the beginning of July, the 45-day festival makes use of every available space in town for a long list of concerts and theatrical performances that take place in every courtyard, square and bastion. In 1952, Marko Fotez, one of the original group of enthusiasts who started the festival, brought a production of *Hamlet* to the Lovrijenac Fort, and this soon became the favoured setting for the famous Shakespearean classic. The Renaissance-baroque architecture of the town has, over the years, provided equally appropriate backdrops for many classic works such as Goethe's *Iphigenia*, which was staged in Gradac Park by the great Croatian director Branko Gavella, and Vojnović's *The Trilogy of Dubrovnik*, set in the authentic rooms of the Rector's Palace. And dance companies such as Alvin Ailey, Merce Cunningham and Martha Graham have set their pieces in historical locations such as the terrace of the Revelin Fort.

Tickets for the headliner events usually sell out well in advance, so anyone planning to attend should check out the festival website (Ⓦ www.dubrovnik-festival.hr) as soon as the programme becomes available, usually in April. For some of the smaller performances, there are usually tickets available at the festival kiosks on Stradun and at the Pile Gate. It's also a good idea to book accommodation very early since the town fills up quickly at festival time. For more information Ⓣ 020 412 288 or Ⓔ program@dubrovnik-festival.hr

History

If Dubrovnik knows one thing well, it is that beauty has its price.
Almost from its founding in the 7th century, Dubrovnik (formerly
known as Ragusa) has been forced to pay off potential conquerors –
and indeed has done right up to the 20th century – in order to
preserve its internal autonomy or save the city from destruction.
Byzantine emperors, Venetian doges, Normans, Hungarians, Turks:
all demanded tribute of one sort or another as a price of going away
and leaving Dubrovnik alone.

By dealing deftly with warring powers, by the 15th and 16th
centuries Dubrovnik was experiencing a Golden Age with a
merchant fleet that ranked third in the world and a ruling class
that spent lavishly on the arts. However, when the great earthquake
of 1667 either totally destroyed or badly damaged every building in
the city, Dubrovnik was already experiencing a downturn in its
prosperity; by now England and Holland dominated the seas and
trade had shifted to the Americas. There was massive chaos after
the quake as people fled in panic rather than trying to control fires.
It was said that pupils were heard crying for help from beneath
the rubble of their school, and there was looting and pillaging
everywhere. When the city was finally rebuilt, it was in the white
stone that dominates today rather than the elaborately wealthy
Renaissance style of before. For the next two centuries Dubrovnik
was caught between adversaries, as the Hapsburg Empire battled
with the Turks and Napoleon with Russia, each empire crashing in
its turn.

When the Hapsburg Empire was finally pulled apart in 1918,
Dubrovnik was incorporated into the newly created Yugoslavia. This
hobbled along through recessions and hardships until World War II,

when Communist partisans became the only effective force against the Axis occupation. After Dubrovnik was liberated in 1944, it became part of the Republic of Croatia, a semi-autonomous unit within Yugoslavia under Marshall Tito. Here it remained until the final collapse of Communism in 1989.

In 1991, with the United States refusing to recognise Croatian independence and Serbia pushing for a unified Yugoslavia, war once again broke out. The Yugoslav army began its attack on Dubrovnik on 1 October, overrunning tourist resorts in the south, shelling targets within the city and destroying the airport and the seaport at Gruz. The bombardment lasted until May 1992 when finally, once again, Dubrovnik's beauty saved the day. Since the city had been declared a World Heritage site and its city walls recognised as Europe's best, there was a huge global outcry at this terrible destruction. The attacking forces retreated, but they left behind a city with almost all of its hotels damaged in one way or another, and much of the rest scarred from mortars or shelling.

Dubrovnik has now been 'back in business' for several years, slowly whittling away at the immense debt incurred from the war. Working together with UNESCO, the authorities have repaired and rebuilt all damaged buildings, recreating the magnificent jewel in the crown of Croatia.

Lifestyle

Croats see themselves as belonging to the Western world, even though in terms of religion the country stands between Islam and Orthodox Christianity in the East and the Catholicism of central Europe. The official language, according to the Constitution, is Croat,

● *Young Croatians regard themselves as Western Europeans*

but in the large cities and along the coast most people speak at least one foreign language (usually German), although English is coming into wider usage, particularly among younger people.

When meeting a Croatian, it's usual to shake hands, although a kiss on the cheek is appropriate when it's a friend. Croatians tend to be friendly but not obsequious – shopkeepers and waiters are not universally helpful. In conversations, tread carefully when the 1991 war comes up: it can be a conversational minefield, since years of intermarriage has blurred any clear dividing lines between Serb and Croat.

As a visitor, casual clothing when sightseeing and on the beaches is usual, but churches frown on anything scanty – legs and shoulders should be covered, even if it's just for a quick look inside a church. For business, appearance is important: this means a suit and tie for men and business dress for women. Restaurants and nightclubs don't require this kind of formality, but Croatians always try to look their best when eating out so it's wise to follow suit. One place where you don't have to worry about dress is at one of the many nudist beaches (these have signs with the letters FKK on them). At family beaches, it is OK to go topless, except when going into a beachside bar or restaurant, when tops should be worn.

When it comes to food, Croatians usually eat lunch relatively late in the afternoon, so restaurants have a kind of daily brunch called *marende* available in the morning. (It's similar to lunch but with smaller portions.) Pizzerias, perhaps as a legacy from the years of Venetian rule, are everywhere, and no Croatian town is without one. Another legacy, this time from Hapsburg rule, is a love of pastries. Local *slastičarnice* (patisseries) are filled with tortes and rolls and lots of goodies stuffed with whipping cream. At meal times, Croatians clink glasses and look directly into each other's eyes.

Culture

Having experienced hundreds of years of foreign occupation, Croatia has a rich and multifaceted cultural heritage that has left Greek and Roman ruins overlaid with later layers of Venetian Gothic and Hapsburg splendour. This influence is seen clearly in the architecture and cathedrals, particularly in the work of such sculptors as Juraj Dalmatinac of Zadar in the 15th century. His outstanding cathedral of St Jacob in Sibenik has apses that feature the faces of local people. Dalmatian artists worked closely with Italian artists, adopting the Italian Renaissance style, and much of their work sits today in international museums. Also of Dalmatian origin was the 20th-century sculptor Ivan Meštrović, whose simple, emotionally powerful work won him many admirers, including Rodin. A large collection of his sculptures can be seen at his former home in Zagreb.

In classical music, Croatia has produced many excellent musicians. Perhaps the most famous is the 18th-century composer Franz Joseph Haydn, who was born in a Croatian sector of Austria. His music is largely influenced by folk melodies, an area in which Croatia makes its most original musical contribution to the world of music.

Croatian literature, like its art, was strongly influenced by the Italian Renaissance and flowered in the Dalmatian region. One of Dubrovnik's most famous writers, Ivan Gundulić, was born in the late 16th century. He is considered Croatia's greatest poet. His epic poem, *Osman*, which celebrates the Polish victory over the Turks in 1621, is a Croatian classic. The plays of 16th-century playwright

○ Croatia is proud of its musical heritage

Marin Držić (after whom the theatre in Dubrovnik is named) are still performed and enjoyed today. Among more contemporary writers, Miroslav Krleža is a giant: a novelist and playwright whose books have been translated into English. Ivo Andrić, born in Bosnia of Croatian parents, won the Nobel Prize for literature in 1961 for his work, which includes *The Bridge on the Drina* (1945).

Dubrovnik's annual highlight is the Summer Festival when the whole town becomes a stage. International figures in the worlds of opera and music come to perform at the 45-day festival that culminates in a huge fireworks display. The cultural scene for the rest of 'the season' (roughly May to October) is equally rich: Dubrovnik has its own symphony orchestra, theatre groups and dance ensembles. The indefatigable symphony performs year-round in a number of venues, such as the Revelin Fortress, just outside the Ploče Gate, and the Church of Our Saviour just inside the Pile Gate. Throughout the summer there are impromptu open-air rock and jazz performances.

Folk dancing and folk music are tremendously popular with young and old alike. Dubrovnik has one of the country's most famous troupes – the 300-strong Lindo ensemble. On Sundays from May to October there are also regular traditional dances and bands playing in front of St Blaise's Church. One special folk-dance show is staged in the village of Čilipi, 25 km (15½ miles) south of Dubrovnik, on Sundays after mass.

▶ *The Romanesque arches of the Franciscan Monastery cloisters*

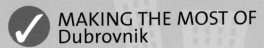

MAKING THE MOST OF
Dubrovnik

Shopping

As a shopping destination, Croatia is not the trendiest place, but does produce some interesting items that are good to take home as gifts or for your store-cupboard. Croatia has had a long tradition of skilled handicraft production, and the best of this is the lace work and embroidery. The embroidery is found almost everywhere: a characteristic design in a red stitching on a white background, used on table linens, pillowcases and blouses. Pag lace is the most famous in the country, which uses a skill dating back to the Renaissance. The lace is made on a long cylindrical cushion by lace-makers who interpret designs handed down through the generations.

Lavender and other herbs made into fragrant oils or bound into sachets make a good and inexpensive gift. Some of the best lavender products come from the island of Hvar. Another good (if heavy) gift are the stone products from the island of Brač, which are usually in the form of candlesticks, ashtrays or vases. Penkala writing instruments (named after Eduard Penkala, the Croatian inventor of the first mechanical pencil and the first solid-ink fountain pen) can be found in most stationery stores and tourist shops, as can cravats – Croatia just happens to be the home of the cravat.

Some of the best souvenirs tend to be edible or drinkable, particularly wines and speciality liqueurs such as Bremet liquor or brandies with herbs in the bottles. Croatian wines are not well known abroad, mainly because they are produced in such small quantities, but they are surprisingly good; as is rakija, a distilled spirit made from a grape base that is normally drunk as an aperitif or digestive. Among the white wines, a good choice is Posip and Grk (from Korčula), Vugava, Malvazija and Traminac. For reds, try the Dingač, Plava and Babić.

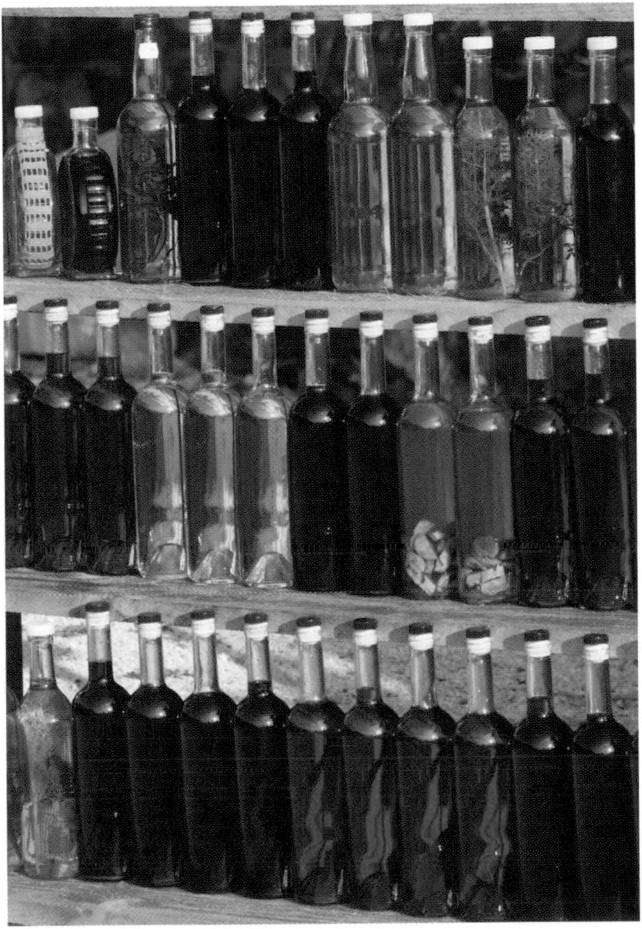

Croatian liqueurs make a delicious, drinkable souvenir

Cheeses are excellent, particularly those from the island of Pag, but be sure to get them in sealed packages or they may be confiscated at Customs. Croatian truffles (*tartufi*) and truffle-based products (like oils) are a good buy, as are herbal teas, which are usually available freshly dried in the markets. If you're driving, buy some onions – the sweet, sweet onions of Croatia are a very special treat. Ajvar is another taste sensation: a red, creamy paste made of ripe red peppers that is wonderful on sandwiches. You can buy it in jars. For the sweet tooth, Paprenjak is a traditional aromatic pastry

USEFUL SHOPPING PHRASES

What time do the shops open/close?
Kada se zatvaraju otvaraju/trgovine?
Ka-da se `zat-va-ra-yoo ot-va-ra-yoo/tr- `go-vine?

How much is this?	**Can I try this on?**
Koliko je to?	Mogu li to probati?
`Ko-li-ko ye to?	*Mo-goo li to `pro-ba-ti?*

My size is ...	**I'll take this one, thank you**
Moj broj je...	Hvala, uzet ću ovo
Moy broy ye...	*Hva-la oo-zet choo o-vo*

This is too large/too small/too expensive.
Do you have any others?
Ovo je preveliko/premalo/ preskupo. Imate li nešto drugo?
O-vo ye `pre-ve-li-ko/`pre-ma-lo/`pre-skoo-po. `I-ma-te li ne-shto droo-go?

made of honey, walnuts and pepper that even comes in specially designed boxes or bags.

TIE ONE ON

Of all the millions of businessmen who knot their ties each morning, few realise that the wearing of a tie actually began in Croatia. It all started in the early 17th century, when Croatian soldiers started wearing narrow scarves tied loosely around the neck. When foreign soldiers came to Paris during the Thirty Years War, among them were Croatian mercenaries who were wearing their scarves. The Croatian's stylish neckties impressed the French, always on the lookout for a fashion statement, so by 1650 neckwear '*à la croate*' had hit the court of Louis XIV. This phrase evolved into *la cravate*. Not long after, King Charles II, in exile in France, fell in love with the style. When he returned to England he took it with him as the height of culture and elegance.

⬤ *Woven throws are among the range of handicrafts on offer*

Eating & drinking

When it's mealtime, look for a *restoran*, *restauracija* or *konoba* (tavern) – the décor may vary but the food will be much the same. A *gostiona* (inn) is a more basic version of a *restoran*. For Croatians, the most important meal of the day is lunch (ručak) which they eat relatively late in the afternoon. For visitors, lighter meals (low-cost smaller portions) are available during the *marende*, a kind of brunch snack, between 10.30 and noon.

For a picnic lunch, the nearest open-air market or *samoposluga* (supermarket) will carry the bread, cheese, meats, fruit and vegetables that you need. Bread can be bought at a *pekarnica* (bakery) and sandwiches can often be made up or on request. *Burek* is a delicious Croatian pastry filled with cheese, which makes a good quick snack, or you can try grilled kebabs served in a *somun* (a flat bread bun).

In Dubrovnik, and all along the Dalmatian coast, plain, grilled seafood dishes are the big favourite; all are seasonal and supremely fresh. The classic is grilled fish served with olive oil and lemon with *blitva sa krumpirom* (swiss chard and potatoes with garlic and olive oil) as an accompaniment. Another favourite is shellfish *na bužaru* (quickly cooked with white wine, garlic and parsley). One shellfish not to miss, particularly if you get to Mali Slon, is *ostrige* (oysters) or *dagnje* (mussels) – you won't find them fresher or more tasty anywhere.

Croatians like to serve their cheese first, before the main meal, often with *pršut*, a home-cured ham from Istria or Dalmatia. This typical and delicious delicacy goes through a long process of cleaning, salting, hanging and smoking; it will melt in your mouth. *Paški sir* comes from the island of Pag and is a hard, piquant cheese

RESTAURANT CATEGORIES

Price ratings are for a basic meal of main course, salad and a drink.

£ 30–60 Kn   ££ 60–100 Kn   £££ 100–150 Kn

that has a taste somewhere between Parmesan and mature cheddar. Soups are usually clear and light and served with very thin noodles.

For main courses, grilled or pan-fried chops are popular, and come either plain or as a schnitzel (*bečki odrezak*), or stuffed with cheese and ham. *Mjesano meso* (mixed grill) is on most menus and consists of pork or veal cutlet, a few rissoles of minced meat and perhaps some spicy *kobasica* (sausage). Lamb is often prepared as a spit-roast; you can sometimes see a whole lamb being cooked beside the restaurant. Stews reflect the central European heritage, with *gulaš* (goulash) done as a sauce over pasta and *pašticada* (beef in vinegar, wine and prunes). Italian-influenced risottos are a popular accompaniment to the main course, especially 'black risotto' made with squid ink.

For dessert, try a Dubrovnik speciality called *rožata*, the local crème caramel. Other typical desserts include *sladoled* (ice cream), *torta* (cake) and *palčinke* (pancakes, which are usually served with marmalade, walnuts or chocolate sauce).

Most restaurants serve wine by the glass, carafe or bottle, while *kavanas* have a full range of alcoholic and non-alcoholic drinks as well as pastries and ice creams. A *kafic* is a smaller version of a *kavana* and usually caters to a younger crowd. Cafés and café-bars open early for that mandatory morning espresso and start serving

m 09.00. The usual closing time is 23.00, although they
...es stay open later in the summer. Pubs tend to look a bit
...; they serve both local and imported beers. Croatian beers are
...ally high quality – two good local brands are Ožujsko and
...arlovačko, or Tomislav, which is a domestic dark beer. Croatian
wines, both red and white, are good, with the best of them being
from the Pelješac peninsula or from Korčula (try the fruity dry
whites from Posip and Grk). Prosek is a sweet wine, tawny red in
colour, which is usually chilled with an ice cube or two. *Travarica* is a
strong grappa flavoured with herbs, while *slivovica* (brandy) is made
from plums.

Service charges aren't usually included in the bill, so the
common practice (as when paying for a taxi, too) is to round up the
bill to the nearest ten kuna or so. If the service has not been good,
then it's up to you whether you tip or not.

🔺 *Enjoy the café culture of the city*

USEFUL DINING PHRASES

I would like a table for ... people
Trebam stol za .... osoba
Tre-bam stol za ...`o-so-ba

May I have the bill, please?
Platiti, molim?
`Pla-ti-ti mo-lim?

Waiter!/Waitress!
Konobar!/Konobarica!
Ko-no-bar!/ko-no-ba-ri-tsa!

Could I have it well-cooked/medium/rare, please?
Molim vas za mene dobro pečeno/polupečeno/na
engleski način?
*Mo-lim vas za me-ne do-bro pe-che-no/`po-loo-pe-che-no/na
`en-gle-ski na-chin?*

I am a vegetarian. Does this contain meat?
Ja sam vegetarijanac. Da li ovo ima mesa?
Ya sam ve-ge-ta-ri-ya-nats. Da li ovo ima me-sa?

Where is the toilet (restroom) please?
Molim vas, gdje je WC?
Mo-lim vas gdie ye ve tse?

I would like a cup of/two cups of/another coffee/tea
Molim jednu/dvije/još jednu kavu/jedan/dva/još jedan čaj
*Mo-lim yed-noo/dvie/yosh yed-noo ka-voo/ye-dan/dva/yosh
ye-dan chay*

Entertainment & nightlife

In a city that wraps itself around a seasonal tourist population, the big entertainment events are naturally staged in the warm summer months, the most notable being the huge Dubrovnik Summer Festival (see page 12). Adding to the rich cultural environment, there are informal open-air pop and jazz concerts in the Old Town during the high season, and special events at the town's two main cultural institutions – the **Marin Držić Theatre**, which specialises in serious drama (though note that the productions are in Croatian), and the **Dubrovnik Symphony**, which holds concerts year-round. The most common venues are the **Church of Our Saviour** (Sveti Spas) just inside the **Pile Gate** for candlelit performances, and the **Revelin Fortress** just outside the **Ploče Gate**. Tickets for the symphony can be bought from the DSO office on Starčićeva 29.

🔺 *There are plenty of lively bars in the Old Town*

Croatia has a lengthy tradition in folk dancing and Dubrovnik's most famous troupe is the 300-person Linđo ensemble. They perform twice a week from May to October at the Lazareti in the summer months (check with the tourist office or your hotel concierge for times). The Marin Držić Theatre, beside the Rector's Palace, presents plays, but largely in Croatian. Tickets are sold at the theatre and they are inexpensive.

The **Kino Sloboda** is the main cinema and has recently been renovated; there's also **Kino Jadran** nearby. In Lapad, **Kino Lapad** and **Kino Slavica** are both open-air theatres, only open during the summer months. (The word *kino* in Croat means 'theatre'.) Most films are subtitled rather than dubbed into Croatian, and tickets are cheap. However, make sure you look for films made in English-speaking countries, or you may find yourself listening to characters speaking Russian with Croatian subtitles.

The best selection of bars are in the Old Town, with many of them prominent on the popular marbled streets. Wander down some of the labyrinthine alleys to find some of the more interesting and less typical bars. The Old Town is lively at night with lots of music played in the cafés, especially during the summer season, but actual 'night life' is a bit thinner on the ground. **Lazareti**, out past the Ploče Gate, has the hippest music, DJs and dancing – they occasionally organise live rock, jazz and ethno gigs as well. The hottest spot in town is probably the mainstream disco, **Latino Club Fuego**, which stays open on Thursday to Saturday from 23.00 to 04.00, one of the few places open through the early hours. There are discos in most major hotels during the summer months, while some city clubs transfer to the open air at coastal resorts during the summer. There's not much information in the local press on events, so the best bet is to ask around or look for posters in town.

Sport & relaxation

SPECTATOR SPORTS

Water polo is the number one sport in Dubrovnik, and watching VK Jug, one of the world's best water-polo clubs, is a very popular pastime among Croatians. A league called Divlja Liga plays during the summer, with each team representing one of Dubrovnik's beaches. Half serious, half fun, this is for amateurs only and everyone can join in. If you want to play, contact the attendants on your beach.

Football

As in the rest of Croatia, **football** (*nogomet*) is keenly followed in Dubrovnik. There's a local team called HNK Gošk that was put together recently by a Dubrovnik entrepreneur. They usually play in the small Lapad Stadium at weekends.

PARTICIPATION SPORTS

Hiking is one of the best ways of checking out the beautiful countryside around Dubrovnik. The path above Šipcine will take you up to the top of **Mount Srd** for an amazing view of the whole archipelago. Other good hikes include several at Župa and on the Pelješac peninsula. Croatia has had a long **climbing** tradition and was among the first seven nations in the world to found a national climbing organisation. For more information contact the Croatian Climbing Federation ⓐ A Kozarčeva 22 in Zagreb ① 014 823 624

On a sunny day with the ocean breezes blowing, the place to be is in Konavle, where they have a number of small horse ranches. Blue Trail Horseback Riding organises five-hour treks along the

Adriatic coastline, led by an experienced trainer. Popovice ☎ 020 798 899, ask for Mr Pero Kojan.

With such great lakes and warm coastal water, **water sports** are big in Croatia – **windsurfing**, **fishing**, **scuba diving** (see page 101), **sailing**, **rowing**, **water polo**, and **kayaking**. A number of companies, such as Aurora Maris (ⓐ A Metohijska 2 ☎ 020 313 445), have fleets of charter boats for bareboat or skippered sailing. For detailed information, contact the tourist office. For fishermen, there's everything from big game fishing to fly fishing, but a licence is required (for details call the Ministry of Agriculture, ⓐ A M. Majoriće 4 ☎ 020 332 393).

Lovers of more extreme sports might want to try **paintball**, or even **bungee-jumping** from the elegant Franco Tudman suspension bridge. You don't have to book, just turn up with your courage any time between 1 May and 1 October. It's near the modern port of Dubrovnik, west of the Old Town in the suburb of Gruž. For details, call Luci Bilic, ☎ 020 418 516

There are two **fitness centres** in Dubrovnik: Fiziofitness Lapad ⓐ A Kardinala Stepinca 18 ☎ 020 436 899 and Wellness Dalmacija ⓐ Zlatni potok 24 ☎ 098 164 5269

🔺 *The clear waters of the Adriatic*

Accommodation

Dubrovnik has been in the hotel business in one form or another since 1347, and has survived through many vicissitudes. During the siege of Dubrovnik, however, the city lost around half of its hotel availability, both through the bombing and later because refugees had to be housed. The accommodation situation is improving fast now, though, and most hotels have been repaired and reopened.

If you want to stay right in the city centre, there is not a great deal of choice in terms of inexpensive accommodation. There are excellent options outside the Old Town, though, and these are at most a short walk or bus ride away from the centre. If money is no object, there are some great places overlooking the sea just east of the town walls; while in the mid-range there are a number of options on the Lapad Peninsula, about 3 km (1¾ miles) from the centre, or in the Gruž port area. If you have access to a car, you can look at some of the pension-style places in the villages around Dubrovnik. The best bet for good standard accommodation close to town is to book a room or apartment through an agency. Most of these are self-catering.

During the summer season, especially from June to September, there's a big demand for rooms, especially by tour groups who block-book, so independent travellers should ring well in advance of arrival to be assured of a room. Prices in the highest season (July and August) can be 20 per cent or more higher than winter or off-season rates.

● *The Argentina has lovely views towards Dubrovnik Old Town*

❶ A word of warning: anyone arriving via ferry or bus is likely to be swamped with offers of unlicensed rooms, and while some of these may turn out to be OK, others may be a long way from the centre of town and have all sorts of hidden 'extra costs' associated – so be careful.

Some websites that may be useful:
ⓦ www.dubrovnik-online.com ⓦ www.dubrovnik-apartments.com
ⓦ www.dubrovnik-gallery.com ⓦ www.dubrovnik-area.com

HOTELS & GUEST HOUSES

Ohran £ Small, 11-room hotel with basic but spotless rooms. Nice location in a quiet cove below a fortress. Good restaurant. ⓐ Od Tabakarije 1, near Old Town ❶ 020 414 183

Zagreb £ Great value in this small 2-star hotel with clean rooms in a lovely refurbished old building ⓐ Šetalište kralja Zvonimira 27 Lapad ❶ 020 436 146

Lapad ££ Once a graceful summer villa, this large hotel has good basic rooms and public areas that echo its former life. Small swimming pool. ⓐ Lapadska obala 37 ❶ 020 432 922 or 413 576 ⓦ www.hotel-lapad.hr

PRICE RATINGS
Gradings used in this book are based on cost per person for two people sharing the least expensive double room with ensuite bathroom and breakfast in high season (July & August).
£ Under 200 Kn ££ 200–500 kn £££ above 500 kn

Neptun ££ On the Babin Kuk, this ten-storey building has south-facing rooms, most with a sea view. Its bright, self-contained, airy rooms are good for families. Near the beach. ⓐ Kardinala Stepinca 31 ⓣ 020 440 100 ⓦ www.hotel-neptun.hr

Stari Grad ££ Recently renovated, this charming little hotel within the city walls has only eight rooms, but it also has a superb upper terrace where you can eat your breakfast while enjoying panoramic views over the bay in the summer. ⓐ Od Sigurate 4 ⓣ 020 321 373/322 244 ⓦ www.hotelstarigrad.com

Argentina £££ This is another recently renovated 5-star hotel with a swimming pool and beach area. It has fine views towards Dubrovnik Old Town and is within walking distance of the centre. ⓐ Frana Supila 14 ⓣ 020 440 555 ⓦ www.hoteli-argentina.hr

Excelsior £££ This is a 5-star hotel with all the trimmings – again, recently remodelled – and within easy walking distance of the Old Town. There are great views from the vast terrace that leads off the restaurant and the bar. Ask for rooms in the old part of the hotel, and preferably go for the ones with a balcony facing the sea. ⓐ Frana Supila 12 ⓣ 020 353 353 ⓔ info@hotel-excelsior.hr ⓦ www.hotel-excelsior.hr

Hilton Imperial £££ Just a few steps away from the Pile Gate, this new, 5-star hotel, which was created out of two 19th-century palaces, has all the comforts and conveniences you will need, including a terrace and indoor swimming pool. The hotel has an interesting history: it was closed for a decade after the 1991 shelling of Dubrovnik; such notables as George Bernard Shaw and H.G. Wells stayed in its former incarnation. ⓐ Marijana Blaz 2, Old Town ⓣ 020 320 320 ⓦ www.hilton.com

Pucić Palace £££ Once an 18th-century palace belonging to the Pucić family, this is now a completely renovated 5-star hotel standing right on the main market square within the city walls. Plush and fully equipped. ⓐ Od Puča 1 ⓣ 020 324 111 ⓦ www.the pucicpalace.com

Villa Dubrovnik £££ Just east of the centre, this small hotel built into a cliff is intimate. It has a beautiful restaurant overlooking the Old Town. The walk into town takes about 15 minutes, or you can use the hotel boat. Has its own rocky beach. ⓐ Vlaha Bukovca 6 ⓣ 020 422 933 ⓦ www.villa-dubrovnik.hr

YOUTH HOSTEL & PRIVATE ROOMS

Youth Hostel £ Between Gruz and the Old Town, this hostel has bunk-bed accommodation in four- to six-person dormitories. Basic breakfast on the terrace or kitchen facilities, but call in advance because it books up quickly in the summer. ⓐ Just off bana Jelacica at V. Sagrestana 3 ⓣ 020 423 241 ⓔ Dubrovnik@hfhs.hr

Private rooms

There is a huge supply of private rooms in Dubrovnik, and these can offer very good value for money as a budget option if you want to stay right in the centre. Dubrovnik travel agencies can be contacted by email to book a room, or you can check a number of online resources (try ⓦ www.dubrovnik-apartments.com). Some of the private agencies that will book are: **Atlas** ⓐ Brsalje 17, near the Pile Gate ⓣ 020 442 574/565 or 442 222 ⓔ call.centre@atlas.hr

Ⓦ www.atlas-croatia.com. Also **Kompas Travel** ⓐ Šveti Dominik 7
Ⓣ 020 322 191 Ⓔ dubrovnik@kompas-travel.com
Ⓦ www.kompas-travel.com

CAMPING

Dubrovnik, at the time of writing, only has one campsite: the
Auto-Camp Solitudo, managed by the Babin Kuk complex. It
has 238 pitches, a pool, restaurant and tennis courts, as well as
newly refurbished bathrooms and laundry areas. Ⓛ 1 April to 1 Nov.
Ⓣ 020 448 686; Ⓦ www.babinkuk.com. A little further out there
are camp sites in Trsteno (Ⓣ 020 751 060), Kupari (Ⓣ 020 485 548)
and Srebreno (Ⓣ 020 487 078).

⬤ *The Excelsior's magnificent sea view*

THE BEST OF DUBROVNIK

A city break in Dubrovnik will soothe your senses. Here you can enjoy the beauty of an ancient walled city, the startlingly clear blue waters of the Adriatic, the taste of superb fresh seafood and the sound of silence.

TOP 10 ATTRACTIONS

- **Tour the city walls** This aerial promenade of Europe's best city walls has panoramic views of the Adriatic and glimpses of the rooftops and alleyways of the town (see page 58).

- **Take a look at the Franjevačka Samostan (Franciscan Monastery)** Home to Croatia's most beautiful medieval cloister, the friary also has a history as a pharmacy dating back nearly 700 years (see page 60).

- **Visit Korčula** This verdant island provides a taste of traditional Croatian life and has an attractive town with a Venetian flavour (see page 76).

- **Take a boat trip to Cavtat** Once the ancient city of Epidaurum, this is now a charming, palm-fringed resort (see page 88).

- **Order a glass of wine** and sit above the rocks outdoors at Cafe Buža watching the sun set.

- **Take a ferry to Mljet** and enjoy the peace and quiet of the vast national park (see page 98).

- **Head to Stradun**, the main street that is at the heart of action in Dubrovnik, and spend a morning window-shopping, sipping cappuccino, and watching the world stroll by.

- **Enjoy an ultra-fresh fish dinner at the old port** You won't taste fresher fish anywhere than at a restaurant right next to the fish market (see page 72–3).

- **Journey to the Elaphite Islands** Among the Adriatic coast's beautiful sandy beaches, these have the cleanest and clearest water (see page 92).

- **Sample the oysters of Mali Ston** For lovers of seafood, this is an unmissable treat (see page 105).

The Rector's Palace, once the heart of the Ragusa Republic

Your at-a-glance guide to seeing and experiencing the best of Dubrovnik, depending on the time you have available.

HALF-DAY: DUBROVNIK IN A HURRY

With only a half a day to spare, the best move is to lace up some walking shoes and start with one of Dubrovnik's key selling points: the 2 km (1¼ mile) walk around the city walls. You'll get sea views to the island of Lokrum and a great cityscape of the Old Town. Take a look at the Pile Gate, and then have an espresso or drink on the lovely terrace of the Kavana Dubravka, right outside the gate. Visit the superb baroque Katedrala and, if there's time, head down the Stradun and check out Europe's oldest continuously operating pharmacy in the Franjevačka Samostan (Franciscan Monastery).

1 DAY: TIME TO SEE A LITTLE MORE

In addition to the sites suggested for the half-day tour, the Dominikanski Samostan (Dominican Monastery), with its stunning Renaissance pieces, is highly recommended. A tour of the Stradun is also very enjoyable, with a checklist of the Old Town's best historic sights, such as Velika Onofrijeva Fontana (Onofrio's Great Fountain) and the Sinagoga (Synagogue). St John's Fortress houses the Pomorski Muzej (Maritime Museum), which gives an overview of Dubrovnik's seafaring past. If it's very hot, then why not take a taxi-boat to the island of Lokrum and enjoy an afternoon of swimming and relaxing on the beaches there?

2–3 DAYS: SHORT CITY BREAK

After spending the first day of your break in the Old Town, take a trip to the Elaphite Islands, a short ferry-ride from Dubrovnik. The islands were a popular summer retreat for Ragusan nobles, and hiking through the pine woods with the scent of rosemary and sage in the air is a real delight. The three principal islands in the group, Koločep, Lopud and Šipan, each have their own special quality, but all have sleepy villages surrounded by olive groves and grape vines. Koločep has a good sandy beach for swimming in the clear Adriatic Sea. You can overnight here and explore all three islands, or spend the third day in Cavtat, a charming fishing village set in a stunning bay around 30-minutes' boat ride from Dubrovnik. There are some interesting sights here, such as the Račić Mausoleum or the Vlaho Bukovac Gallery. The best beaches are in a bay east of the town centre.

LONGER: ENJOYING THE AREA TO THE FULL

With more time, a day or two on Korčula provides a stunning diversion. A lush island covered in vineyards and ancient buildings, Korčula was the birthplace of Marco Polo in 1254. A 'big city' visit to Split is also recommended, to take in the Roman ruins and history. For seafood-lovers, a stop in Ston to sample mouth-watering, ultra-fresh oysters is also a must.

Something for nothing

In Dubrovnik, the best things in life really are free: the views, the architecture, the sheer beauty of the town itself. Churches, cathedrals and monasteries abound in Dubrovnik and admission fees are usually nominal. **Crkva Svetog Vlaha**, the baroque church dedicated to the city's patron saint, St Blaise, contains a statue of him holding an early model of the city. There's also a lone 15th-century **Sinagoga** (synagogue) on Žudioska Street; the second

⬤ *The magnificent Great Fountain of Onofrio*

oldest of its kind in Europe: it contains 17th-century furnishings, Torah scrolls and other artifacts from a once flourishing Jewish community.

Indoor and outdoor markets are high on the 'free list', and Dubrovnik's two daily ones are always a big draw for photographers. The old market on **Gundulićeva poljana** has everything from vegetables and flowers to fish and lace, while the main city market caters largely for local people. Another good subject for holiday snaps are the fountains in the city – **Velika Onofrijeva Fontana** (Onofrio's Great Fountain) and **Mala Onofrijeva Fontana** (Onofrio's Small Fountain), plus a number of others.

What about testing your balance for free? Just outside the entrance to the **Franjevačka Samostan** (Franciscan Monastery) cloister, there's an unusual stone with a gargoyle face that sticks out from the main wall. The ritual is to stand on this stone, arms outstretched, for as long as possible without falling off.

If you need a break from history, pick up a picnic lunch and head for one of the beaches (like the pebbled Banje beach) for a day of romping in the Adriatic's crystal-clear waters.

The streets themselves offer no end of surprises: you can step out of a church like St Blaise's and find a troupe of entertainers giving a folkloric show, or turn a corner and discover a group of thespians in Renaissance costume shooting a television series. There are also performance spaces and galleries that feature local talent in the stone buildings and courtyards known as the **Lazareti** (once quarantine houses for travellers during the Renaissance).

To end the day, for the price of a glass of sweet Dalmatian wine, you can sit at Buža – an outdoor café perched on the rocks just outside the city's sea-facing walls – and watch the sun sink into the sea.

When it rains

Even though Dubrovnik chalks up a good number of sunny days, it does rain every once in a while, so it's a good idea to save leisurely inspections of the interiors of the city's many churches for a drizzly day. **Crkva Sv Spasa** (St Saviour's) and the **Katedrala** (Cathedral) were both built as 'thank-yous' – the former for deliverance from a storm and the latter for deliverance from an earthquake.

If it's pouring, you can devote plenty of time to discovering the **Franjevačka Samostan** (Franciscan Monastery), with its Romanesque cloister and arches topped with carved human heads and fantastic animals. Fans of the TV series *Cadfael*, the medieval detective-cum-pharmacist monk, will certainly love the pharmacy at the entrance of the monastery – it is actually one of Europe's most famous. Still functioning, it dates back to 1317 and calls itself the oldest pharmacy in Europe.

Damp days are also a good time to hit the galleries in Dubrovnik, and one very good one is **War Photo Limited** (ⓐ A Antuninska 6 ① 020 322 166), which is run by a former war photographer, Wade Goddard. The gallery specialises in first-rate temporary exhibitions that feature the work of the world's greatest war photographers. It's not for the very young or the faint-hearted: War Photo Limited sees itself as an educator in the field of war photography, with a mission statement that aims to look at war 'as it is': raw, frightening and venal. There are several other galleries worth visiting during cloudbursts, including the **Museum of Modern Art**, which features paintings and sculptures by some of Croatia's best artists.

The **Palaca Sponza** (Sponza Palace) is also an enjoyable rainy-day destination. Built in the 16th century, it was originally used as the custom house and mint and stages interesting exhibitions.

Shopping for some Croatian delicacies is also a terrific way to while away any periods of rain. **Franja Coffee & Teahouse** on Od Puca Street in the Old Town has a great selection of olive oils, honey, wild-rose brandy and wine. Don't forget the *pršut*!

🔺 *The fine cloisters of the Franciscan Monastery*

On arrival

TIME DIFFERENCES

Croatia follows Central European Time (CET). During Daylight Saving Time (late Mar–late Sept), the clocks are put ahead one hour. In the Croatian summer, at 12.00 noon, the time is as follows:

Australia Eastern Standard Time 20.00, Central Standard Time 19.30, Western Standard Time 18.00

South Africa 12.00

New Zealand 22.00

UK 11.00

USA and Canada Newfoundland Time 07.30, Atlantic Canada Time 07.00, Eastern Time 06.00, Central Time 05.00, Mountain Time 04.00, Pacific Time 03.00, Alaska 02.00

ARRIVING

By air

Most international flights end in Zagreb with a connection on to Dubrovnik. There are two to three flights a day between the cities and they take one hour. Dubrovnik Airport (☎ 020 773377 ⓦ www.airport-dubrovnik.hr) is around 22 km (13½ miles) east of the city close to the village of Čilipi. A Croatia Airlines airport bus makes regular runs between the airport and the city centre that take about 25 minutes, and there are also taxis readily available. Buses back to the airport leave the bus station 90 minutes before each Croatia Airlines departure. There is no tourist office in the airport, but there is a bank, post office, car-rental office and duty-free shop.

By rail

Croatian Railways (@ Hrvatske željeznice ⓦ www.hznet.hr) serve all major cities except Dubrovnik. For getting around the country, trains are more comfortable than buses and slightly cheaper.

By sea

The ferry terminal is in the port suburb of Gruž, 3 km (1¾ miles) west of Old Town, where year-round overnight ferries (catamarans during the summer) depart for Bari, Italy. These usually depart Bari at 22.00 and arrive in Dubrovnik at 06.00; they leave Dubrovnik at 23.00 and arrive in Bari at 08.00.

By bus

The bus station is about 500 m (¼ mile) south of the ferry terminal. Long-distance buses come straight to the bus station; there is one direct bus a day from Frankfurt, Trieste and Sarajevo. The bus station has Dubrovnik's only left-luggage facility: it is open from ⓛ 04.30 to 21.00 daily ⓣ 060 305 070.

FINDING YOUR FEET

Dubrovnik is compact and easy to navigate once you get a map and see the 'fish skeleton' layout of the streets. Walking around at night is pretty safe, much more so than in many other parts of Europe, and there's little overt crime. One obvious safeguard to take is to lock up any valuable rings and necklaces rather than flaunting them on the streets. The police are visible everywhere, and occasionally they will stop foreigners to ask for identification: be sure you have your passport or identity card with you at all times. The police tend to be helpful, but not all of them speak English.

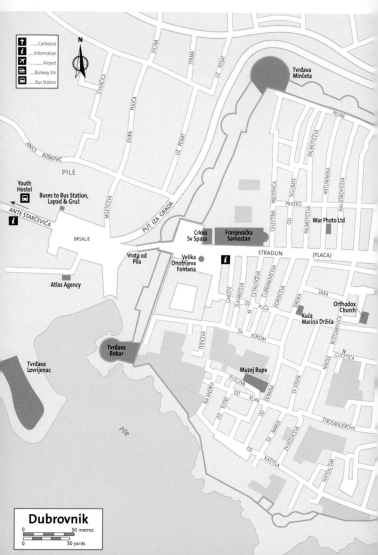

Legend:
- ......Cathedral
- ......Information
- ......Airport
- ......Railway Stn
- ......Bus Station

N

Tvrđava Minčeta

PELINE

PALMOTIĆEVA

ANTUNINSKA

NALJEŠKOVIĆEVA

ŽUDIOSKA

STRMA

UZ POSAT

PUĆA

DURA

MILETIĆEVA

PILE

ANICE BOŠKOVIĆ

Youth Hostel

Buses to Bus Station, Lapad & Gruž

ANTE STARČEVIĆA

BRSALJE

PUT IZA GRADA

MEDOVIĆA

CELESTINA

OD

SIGURATE

PRIJEKO

PALMOTIĆEVA

War Photo Ltd

Crkva Sv Spasa

Franjevačka Samostan

STRADUN   (PLACA)

Vrata od Pila

Velika Onofrijeva Fontana

GARIŠTE

ZLATARIĆEVA

CETALIĆEVA

PUĆA

M

OD

ČUBRANOVIĆEVA

BOŠKOVIĆA

SIROKA

VARA

Orthodox Church

Atlas Agency

FERIĆEVA

ZA ROKOM

Kuća Marina Držića

NIKOLE

BOŽIDAREVIĆA

N

GUČETIĆA

Tvrđava Bokar

MA ANDRIJU

OD

SOTEC

PUŽLJIVA

OD RUPA

DOMINA

Muzej Rupe

SV JOSIPA

Tvrđava Lovrijenac

SV MARIJE

KVIEZDIĆEVA

STROSMAJEROVA

SVETOC SM

OD

KAŠTELA

Pile

Pile

Dubrovnik

0 _____ 50 metres

0 _____ 50 yards

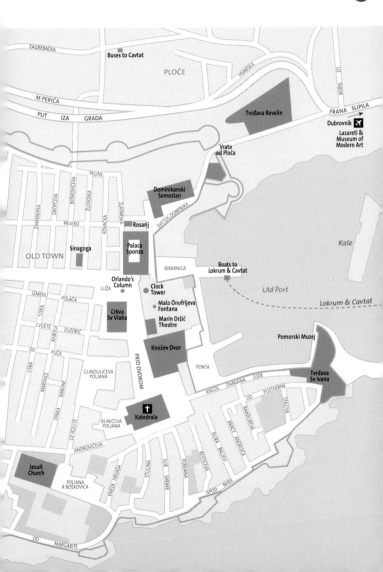

ZAGREBAČKA

Buses to Cavtat

PLOČE

HVARSKA

UZ TABOR

M PERIĆA

FRANA SUPILA

PUT IZA GRADA

Tvrđava Revelin

Dubrovnik ✈
Lazareti &
Museum of
Modern Art

PELINE

Vrata
od Ploča

DROPČEVA

BOŠKOVIĆA

ŽUDIOSKA

ZLATARSKA

KOVAČKA

Dominikanski
Samostan

SVETOG DOMINIKA

ZAMANJINA

PRIJEKO

Rosarij

Kaše

OLD TOWN

Sinagoga

Palaca
Sponza

RIBARNICA

Boats to
Lokrum & Cavtat

Orlando's
Column

LUŽA

Clock
Tower

Stari Port

IZMEĐU

POLAČA

Mala Onofrijeva
Fontana

Lokrum & Cavtat

CVIJETE

KABOGE

ŽUŽORIĆ

Crkva
Sv Vlaha

Marin Držić
Theatre

LIŠKA

PUČA

Knežev Dvor

Pomorski Muzej

OD

MAROJICE

RANJINE

GUNDULIĆEVA
POLJANA

PRID DVOROM

PONTA

KNEZA DAMJANA JUDE

OD PUSTIJERNE

Tvrđava
Sv Ivana

UZ JEZUITE

DINKA

BUNIĆEVA
POLJANA

Katedrala ✝

BANDUREVA

BRAĆE ANDRIĆA

ĐIVA BALEVI

RESTIĆEVA

STJEPKA

ANDROVIĆEVA

Jesuit
Church

POLJANA
R BOŠKOVIĆA

KNEZA HVALA

YNJUIS

ILIJE

ILIJE SARAKE

POBIJANA

ISPOD MIRA

OD MARGARITE

The official language of the country is Croatian, but the majority of younger Croats speak fairly good English, picked up from school and the internet. Most people working in tourism will also have a decent vocabulary, but it doesn't hurt to learn a handful of words and phrases that – at the worst – will raise a laugh. Like anyone, Croatians appreciate a visitor who makes the effort to communicate in the local language.

Women travellers need to know that Croatian society is patriarchal. As in many other southern European countries, Croatian men are quite open with their remarks. Most of these can simply be ignored and the man will generally go away; if he's too persistent,

● *Ferries link the islands to the mainland*

speak firmly and make your intentions to call for help quite clear. Drinking in public areas is fine, but there are bars patronised mainly by men and these should be avoided: a woman alone gives off the wrong signals in this society.

ORIENTATION

Tucked into its walls, Dubrovnik's Old Town is tiny, closed to traffic and easy to navigate around. To enter the city, you have the choice of three gates: the Ponta Gate at the entrance to the harbour; the Pile Gate to the west, by the bus station, and the Ploče Gate to the east. Each of these will lead to the **Stradun** (Placa), the lovely marbled 'main drag' that is only 300 m in length and divides the Old Town

into two. Narrow streets and alleys lead off of the Stradun like ribs from a backbone, and the street is buttressed by two major parallel streets: Prijecko in the north and Od Puca in the south.

Greater Dubrovnik spreads along the Dalmatian coast from the suburb of Ploče in the southeast to the suspension bridge in the northwest, and across the **Lapad** and **Babin Kuk** peninsulas to the west. The main harbour, **Gruž**, sits between the mainland and Babin Kuk. For maps and details, the tourist office at ⓐ Dr Ante Starčevića 7 is open Monday to Saturday from 08.00 to 20.00 in the summer months.

GETTING AROUND

On landing at the newly built Čilipi airport, there are two ways to get into town 20 km (12½ miles) away. For passengers on Croatia Airlines (CA), there's a bus costing about 25 kuna that meets the flight. For departing passengers, buses leave Dubrovnik bus station an hour and a half before the Croatia Airlines departures. For those who are not flying CA, taxis cost around 220 kuna if they are metered and around 200 kuna if you pay cash. For passengers arriving by sea from the port of Gruž, buses (ⓦ No 1A, No 1B and No 3) run from the port to Pile Gate roughly every half-hour. The No 8 bus runs from Ploče hotels to the Ploče Gate. The main bus station in Dubrovnik (intercity and international) is at ⓐ Obala pape Ivana Pavla II 44A ⓣ 060 305 070 or 020 356 987. Local buses cover all of Dubrovnik and run from 05.00 until 12.00 midnight. Tickets are sold at newspaper kiosks or on the bus, but you're expected to have the exact fare (10 kuna at the time of writing). ⓦ www.libertasdubrovnik.hr

Dubrovnik has a good taxi service as well, with stands at the Pile Gate, Gruž, the bus station and Lapad. You can also get someone to call a taxi to pick up at any of the main hotels. As always, you should check to make sure the meter is turned on before you leave, unless you've pre-negotiated the fare to a particular destination.

To go to any of the islands, take one of the local ferries or a taxi-boat – these travel between Dubrovnik's old port and Lokrum every half-hour in the summer. It's a ten-minute crossing. There are also regular boats to and from Cavtat. All other ferries leave from the main quay on Gruž harbour and are usually operated by Jadrolinja (the national ferry company). ⓦ www.jadrolinja.hr

IF YOU GET LOST, TRY ...

Excuse me, do you speak English?
Oprostite, govorite li engleski?
O-`pro-sti-te `go-vo-ri-te li `en-gle-ski?

Can you tell me the way to the bus station/taxi rank/city centre (downtown)/beach?
Možete li mi reći kako mogu doći do/autobusnog kolodvora/taksi-stajalište/centra grada/plaže?
`Mo-zhe-te li mi re-chi ka-ko mo-goo do-chi do` `a-oo-to-boos-nog `ko-lo-dvo-ra/tak-si `sta-ya-li-shta/tsen-tra gra-da/pla-zhe?

Can you point to it on my map?
Možete li mi to pokazati na planu grada?
`Mo-zhe-te li mi to po-`ka-za-ti na pla-noo gra-da?

CAR HIRE

Hiring a car in Dubrovnik is expensive, at around 500 kn a day for an economy car with unlimited mileage. Since the Old Town is so compact for sightseeing, it might not be advisable to rent unless you plan to do some extensive touring around – ferries and buses are a good alternative. The major hire companies have offices in Dubrovnik, but usually you get the best-value rates by booking at home before you leave, either through your airline or on the web. You can try these car-hire companies in the UK:

Autoeurope ☎ 0800 358 1229 ⓦ www.auto-europe.co.uk

Budget ☎ 0870 1539 170 ⓦ www.budget.co.uk

easyCar ☎ 0986 333 3333 ⓦ www.easycar.com

Europcar ☎ 0870 607 500 ⓦ www.europcar.co.uk

Hertz ☎ 0870 844 8844 ⓦ www.hertz.co.uk

▶ *The distinctive red roofs and sturdy walls of Dubrovnik*

Old Town

Dubrovnik's Old Town is compact and the main sights are close to one another, so that you can see them all without any lengthy stops within a couple of hours. If you have a special interest, say in Renaissance art or musical notation, and want to do a thorough exploration, you should allow at least a half a day.

SIGHTS & ATTRACTIONS

City walls

Depending on who you talk to, Dubrovnik's city walls (in purple on the map opposite) are the most beautiful, best-preserved, or most complete city walls in the world. It's certainly the place to start any visit to the city. Wrapping themselves around Dubrovnik for just a little under 2 km (1¼ miles), they measure 25 m (82 ft) at their highest point and 12 m (39¼ ft) at the widest.

The whole circuit can be done in a leisurely hour. Begun in the 8th century, building and repairing went on throughout the centuries, including the extensive work that was carried out on them after the 1991–2 war. There are three entrances onto the walls: one is next to Vrata od Pila (Pile Gate), another on Svetog Dominika leading to the Dominikanski Samostan (Dominican Monastery) and the third on Kneza Damjana Jude near the Akvarij (Aquarium). ◐ 09.00–19.00 in the summer, with shorter hours in the winter

Crkva Sv Spasa (St Saviour's Church) (See map page 50)

Near Onofrio's Great Fountain, this church was erected as the city's 'thank-you' message after it survived the 1520 earthquake. Ironically,

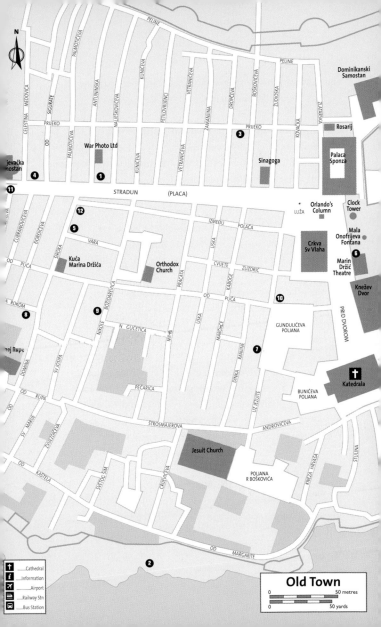

Old Town

0 50 metres

0 50 yards

the façade of this simple Renaissance structure attracts visitors curious about shrapnel damage during the 1991 war.

Dominikanski Samostan (Dominican Monastery)

This old structure, dating back to the early 14th century, has two attractions of major interest: its 15th-century Gothic Renaissance cloister, filled with palm and orange trees, and its museum stuffed with a wealth of Renaissance treasures. Of historical interest, there's a painting of St Blaise holding a model of 16th-century, pre-quake Dubrovnik; a splendid Virgin and Child altarpiece, and a Titian altarpiece of Mary Magdalene and St Blaise. ⓐ off Svetog Dominika 4 ⓣ 020 426 472 ⓛ 09.00–17.00, admission charge

Franjevačka Samostan (Franciscan Monastery)

Beyond the peaceful and beautiful courtyard, the two most interesting parts of the monastery are the cloister and treasury. The capitals in the cloister are decorated with birds, animals and human faces, one of which is rumoured to be the sculptor suffering from a bad toothache. The frescoes in the cloister tell the life of St Francis. The friary is also notable for being the oldest continuously functioning pharmacy in Europe: it was founded in 1317. The treasury has relics from the ancient apothecary's shop as well as manuscripts tracing the history of musical notation. Check out the 'balancing stone' beside the west portal. ⓐ Placa 2 ⓣ 020 321 410 ⓛ 09.00–18.00

Katedrala (Cathedral of the Assumption)

Located right in the heart of the city, the original cathedral was financed, according to legend, by Richard the Lionheart, after he

---

⑩ *Stradun is the main pedestrian artery of the city*

survived a terrible storm just off the coast near Lokrum. At the
height of the storm, the king vowed that – if he survived – he would
build a church. Enterprising Ragusan nobles, on hearing of the
pledge, sent a delegation to Richard, persuading the king that his
money would best be used to build a church in Dubrovnik rather
than Lokrum. ⓐ Kneza Damjana Jude 1 ① 020 323 459
🕐 08.00–20.00 Mon–Sat, 11.00–17.30 Sun

Knežev dvor (Rector's Palace)

Twice blown up by gunpowder stored next door, this version of the
palace dates to the 15th century and once housed all the major
offices of state plus a dungeon (and the gunpowder storage). At the
entrance, you walk through pillars made of Korčula marble, one of
which is said to be of Aesculapius, the god of healing, who was born
in what is now Cavtat. The main door of the palace leads to an
atrium in which summer musical recitals are held.
ⓐ Pred dvorom 1 ① 020 321 437 🕐 09.00–18.00

Mala Onofrijeva Fontana (Onofrio's Small Fountain)

Much daintier than the 'great fountain', this has cherub reliefs and
was carved by the same sculptor. ⓐ Luža Square

Orlando's Column

This doesn't look all that impressive, but when it was built in 1418 it
was the focal point of the city-state, since government ordinances
were promulgated here and punishments carried out. A flag with
the 'Libertas' motto flies from the top and the start of the Dubrovnik
Summer Festival is announced here. The medieval cult of Orlando
(Roland) started in the 12th century and was based on the epic
poem, *Song of Roland*. ⓐ Luža Square

Palaca Sponza (Sponza Palace)

Used as a custom house and mint, the Sponza Palace was built
in the 16th century and grew rapidly as Dubrovnik's wealth
multiplied. It is elaborately carved with Renaissance arches and
Venetian Gothic windows, and currently houses the state archives.
Exhibitions are often held inside the majestic courtyard and,
during the summer festival, there are concerts. A room dedicated
to the defenders who lost their lives during the 1991–92 war
(the Memorial Room of the Defenders of Dubrovnik) is
recommended for history buffs. ⓐ Luža Square ⓒ 08.00–13.00

Stradun (Placa)

This is the city's main street, a 300-m (985-ft) pedestrian zone that
runs from the Pile to the Ploče gates along the line of a channel that
once separated the Roman settlement of Ragusa from the Slavic
settlement of Dubrovnik. Originally paved in the 15th century (and
redone after the earthquake in the 17th), the limestone pavement is
polished with centuries of use, so is shiny and extremely slippery
when wet.

Velika Onofrijeva Fontana (Onofrio's Great Fountain)

(See map page 50)

Just inside the Pile Gate, this fountain, built in 1444, is shaped like
a polygon and was once part of the city's water-supply system.
Topped by a bulbous dome, there are fourteen masks around the
fountain that spout water. Visitors to the city were required to
wash here to guard against bringing in the plague. There were
once statues around the fountain as well, destroyed unfortunately
in the earthquake of 1667. Now the main human forms around
it are teenagers, who like to gather here to chat. ⓐ near Pile Gate

Vrata od Pila (Pile Gate) (See map page 50)
This entrance to the Old Town dates back to 1471 and was
approached across a wooden drawbridge that was pulled up
every night. Today it spans a dry moat with a garden. Just inside
the gate is the first glimpse you get of St Blaise, the city's patron
saint; nearby stands another statue, of famous Croatian sculptor
Ivan Meštrović.

Walking tours

Dubrovnik is an ideal city for walking around, and an hour or two
on the city walls (see page 58) is the best way to start. This tour
takes in the Minčeta, the Revelin, St John's and Bokar fortresses.
Within the old city, there's a good walk, starting outside the Pile
Gate (see above), and ending at the Museum of Modern Art. The
Pile Gate, which dates back to 1471, has a wooden drawbridge that
used to be pulled up every night. Check out the statue to St Blaise
and, further on, one by Ivan Meštrović. From here, head to the
Stradun (see page 63), once a marshy channel that separated
the Roman settlement of Ragusa on one side from the Slavic
Dubrovnik on the other.

Just inside the Pile Gate, spend a bit of time photographing
Onofrio's Great Fountain (see page 63), built in 1444 as part of the
city's plumbing system. The Franjevačka Samostan (Franciscan
Monastery) is next: take a good look at the exterior, but save the
interior for a rainy day. At the far end of the Stradun, Orlando's
Column (see page 62) in Luža Square symbolises the city's desire
for freedom and marked the centre of town when it was built in
1418. On the left-hand side of the square, the Palaca Sponza (Sponza

---

▶ *The city walls are a great vantage point*

Palace) (see page 63) holds the Memorial Room of the Dubrovnik Defenders, the state archives and the original workings of the city clock. The clock tower with its astronomical clock is just behind Orlando's Column. Onofrio's Small Fountain (see page 62), built in 1441, is next to the clock tower. From here, go along the winding Svetog Dominika to the Dominican Monastery (see page 60), out through the Ploče Gate to Lazareti (see page 45), and take a look at the first-class Museum of Modern Art (🄰 Put Frana Fupila 23) 🄣 020 426 590 🄻 10.00–17.00, closed Mon

CULTURE

Dubrovnik Symphony

In continuous performance since 1924, the orchestra has evolved into a fully professional body, spinning off the Dubrovnik City Orchestra and the Dubrovnik Festival Orchestra. It performs in three major concert halls – the Crijević-Pucić Villa, the Rector's Palace, and the interior of the Franciscan church.
🄰 Ante Starčevića 29 🄣 020 417 101 🄦 www.dso.hr

Kuća Marina Držica (Marin Držić House)

This is a theatrical museum, a scientific documentary institute and an exhibition space all rolled into one. It is named in memory of Marin Držić, one of Croatia's greatest playwrights. What makes this museum so unusual is that it's more of a theatrical experience than a museum: visitors find themselves surrounded by puppets, posters and typical stage props. Actors guide people through the exhibits in such a way they feel like participants of a theatrical performance.
🄰 Široka ulica 7 🄣 020 420 490 🄻 09.00–13.00 Mon–Sat and by appointment

Muzej Rupe (Rupe Ethnographic Museum)
This is a glimpse back to the 16th century: an immense stone barn
with fifteen huge storage pits that were used for keeping the
municipal grain. At one time, these pits were dug into floors all over
town, but this is the only one that has survived. The top floor houses
an ethnographic exhibition of rural life and husbandry plus
costumes, textiles and so on.
ⓐ Ulica od Rupa 2 ❶ 020 412 545 ❹ 09.00–19.00 summer;
09.00–14.00 winter

Pomorski Muzej (Maritime Museum) (See map page 50)
Located in St John's Fortress, the Maritime Museum is of great
interest to old salts and those interested in the background of this
seafaring country. It looks at the history of Ragusan sea power, with
model displays of boats throughout the centuries and marine
artefacts. There are trade-route maps, sextants, and a particularly
interesting, well-stocked 19th-century medicine chest, used by
doctors on ships.
❹ 09.00–18.00 in the summer and shorter hours in the winter

RETAIL THERAPY

The main artery for shopping is Stradun (Placa) in the Old Town,
where you'll find clothing and shoe shops in the alleys that run off
the street. There's also a shop where the owner makes and sells
candles. If you are after items that 'say Dubrovnik', the embroidery
distinctive to the Konavle region south of the city is special. You can
find napkins and tablecloths at some of the better gift shops, but
they are pricey. For traditional Croatian jewellery such as filigree
earrings and coral necklaces, try some of the jewellery shops at the

western end of od Puća. Foreigners can claim a sales tax refund within one year for anything they buy. Be sure to ask the salesperson to fill out the tax-refund form when purchasing your goods.

There are two fruit and vegetable markets, one in the Old Town on Gunduliceva poljana and the other one in Gruž. Both sell fresh produce and are open every day until noon – or sometimes longer.

Alogoritam Books This is the best bookshop in town if you've finished that novel you brought and need a new book in English. They also have travel guides and maps. ⓐ Placa 8 ① 020 322044

Arca Antique Shop For collectors or gift-seekers, Arca has a large selection of antique dishes, vases, glasses, tablecloths and paintings by Croatian artists. ⓐ Gundauljeeva poliana

Art Studio 1 Hajdarhodzic Sells handmade clay ships and fishing boats; also some paintings and antiques. ⓐ Zlatarska 1

Aquarius Here's the store to get those souvenirs of Croatian music CDs as well as international music. ⓐ Poljana Paskala 4

Dobrovacka Kuca You can find the best of Croatian wines here, *rakija*, olive oil, truffles and so on. There's a good art gallery upstairs that has featured shows of modern work and Tiffany recently. ⓐ Sv. Dominika 4 ① 020 322 092

◀ *Retail therapy is a must in Dubrovnik*

Euroshop is a department store on Gruska obala, close to the market in Gruž.

Franciscan Monastery Pharmacy For a really unusual gift (and to treat yourself too) stop in at the still-functioning pharmacy to check out the range of unusual lotions and creams, some formulated from recipes dating back to 1317. Some of the recommended are the lemon hand-lotion, rose or lavender face-cream, and the jojoba and menthol moisturiser. If you say it's a gift, they'll give you a special bag. ⓐ In the monastery near the Pile Gate.

Franja Coffee & Teahouse Besides coffee and tea you can pick up great food gifts here too. There's wild-rose brandy, herbal *rakijas* wine made with the local grapes, figs in honey, olive oil and special liqueurs. ⓐ Od Puca 9

Minceta Department Store is in Gruž, 400 m east of the market on Put Republike.

Ronchi hats This hat shop has been around since 1858 and has a rich array of hats that is sure to please hat-lovers. Current owner Marina Ronchi uses the same traditional techniques of hatmaking as her predecessors. ⓐ Lučarića 2, on a narrow lane near Market Square and Orlando monument

Sebastian This art gallery has a large collection of prints for sale, including of paintings by most of the better-known Croatian artists. ⓐ Svetog Dominika 5

TAKING A BREAK

Buffet Škola £ ❶ A family-run sandwich bar that makes delicious *pršut* and cheese sandwiches on homemade bread with locally grown tomatoes. ⓐ Antuninska ulica, a side street between Placa and Pirjeko

Buza £ ❷ Perched on the rocks just outside the Old Town's sea-facing walls, this waterfront bar has atmosphere. Look for the 'cold drinks' sign: serves coffee, travarica, cool beer, lemonade and ice cream. ⓐ On Iza Mira

Don Corleone £ ❸ There are lots of pizza places in town, but for the best slice to take away this has great pizza and other Italian specialties. ⓐ Boškovićeva 4

Festival £ ❹ Was badly damaged during the 1991–2 war, but is now a smart café with the best sticky cakes and Spanish hot chocolate in town. Excellent café breakfast as well. ⓐ Just off the Stradun on Celestina Medovića

Fish Sandwich Bar £ ❺ Has fish and mussel sandwiches for a low-price lunch. ⓐ On Široka Street, next to Proto Restaurant ⓛ 10.00–14.00, 18.00–21.00

Gradska kavana £ ❻ A cavernous café where locals come for cakes and ice cream on the summer terrace or to listen to live piano in the summer. ⓐ Prid Dvorom

AFTER DARK

There are a lot of choices for dinner, with menus that centre around fresh grilled fish, squid and shellfish but with other options as well. The standards are consistently good, but it's better to wander off 'restaurant row' (Prijeko Street), where restaurants offer identical menus and staff use the hard-sell technique. Restaurants are usually open until 23.00, with some extending their hours in the high season. Many of the more popular restaurants require a reservation and make a small cover charge.

Restaurants

You'll be spoilt for choice in terms of restaurants, with the busiest ones being in Old Town along a street called Preko and off Široka Ulica. Some of these are closed in the winter. Menus tend to be similar, with heavy emphasis on seafood, grilled meat, pizza and other Croatian specialities like *rizot* (seafood risotto), *menestra aka* (minestrone soup) and *buzara* (langoustines in a tomato sauce).

Kamenica £ ❼ A no-frills eatery and a favourite of the locals for its simple seafood dishes and fresh oysters. ⓐ Gundulićeva Poljana 8, near the open-air market ● all year but closes at 20.00 in the winter

Mea Culpa £ ❽ A popular restaurant, with good pizza cooked in a wood-fired oven and other Italian dishes at cheap prices. Cosy inside, there are also tables on the street and they have draft Guinness on tap. ⓐ Za Rokom 3 ● 020 424 819 ● 08.00–24.00

Spaghetteria Toni £ ❾ For strong Turkish coffee and what the locals claim is the best pasta (especially the lasagna) in town. Good soups and bruschettas too. ⓐ Božidarevića 14 ⓣ 020 323 134

Marco Polo ££ ❿ Tiny restaurant, but in the summer you can dine in the courtyard on typical dishes such as *crni rižot* (black risotto in cuttlefish ink). A popular hangout for musicians and actors. ⓐ Lučarica 6, on a side street behind the Church of St Blaise ⓣ 020 323 719

Atlas Club Nautika £££ ⓫ Located in a building that once used to be the Dubrovnik Nautical Academy, the building has been renovated and is now considered to be the best place in town for quality seafood. There are grand dining rooms, a small outdoor terrace, formal waiters, crisply folded napkins and an international wine list. ⓐ Brsalje 3 ⓣ 020 442 526/442 573 ⓛ 12.00–24.00

Proto £££ ⓬ Right in the centre of Old Town, Proto has been around since 1886 and is known for its fish specialities prepared from old recipes of Dubrovnik fishermen. Formal dining room with relaxed outdoor terrace and meticulous service. Excellent local wine list. ⓐ Široka ulica 1 ⓣ 020 323 234 ⓛ 11.00–23.00

Bars, clubs & discos

Bebap This is one of the few bars in Old Town to stay open after midnight in the low season as well as high. Occasional live concerts. ⓐ Knez Damjana Jude, the narrow street leading to the Aquarium

Capitano Swings on Friday nights, especially in the summer with a young crowd. ⓐ Pile, just a few steps north of Pile Gate

Divinae Follie On the Lapad Peninsula, this is an open-air disco and the largest club in Dubrovnik. The DJ booth is encircled by the dance floor, which is in turn surrounded by bars. ⓐ Put Vataroslava Lisinskog 56, about a 15-minute drive from Old Town ⓣ 020 435 677

Hard Jazz Café Trubadour Intimate pub that flows out onto the surrounding square in high season. This is owned by a former member of a locally famous 1960s beat group called the Dubrovacki Trubaduri – there is live jazz most nights in the summer. ⓐ Bunićeva poljana

Irish Pub Don't expect wearin' of the green or leprechauns: the Irish ale is as far as it goes. It does have a friendly atmosphere and prices are reasonable, so it's popular with students and tourists. You will probably be able to catch midweek football here. ⓐ Izmedu polaca 5 ⓣ 020 323 992

Latino Club Fuego Probably the most popular club in Dubrovnik, with good music and reasonable prices. ⓐ Brsalje 11, near Pile Gate ⓛ Open until 04.00

Libertina Tiny place and a good spot to meet chatty local people. ⓐ Side street next to Sponza Palace

Old Hospital This is just that: an abandoned hospital that has been turned into a youth hostel and club for the younger crowd. Live bands and DJs and a hardcore beat. ⓐ Dr. Ante Starčevića 41

Otok This is an alternative hangout in Old Town that's been described as 'an after-hours chill-out lounge-cum-speakeasy/art gallery where underground artists and mainstream clubbers co-mingle'. ⓐ Pobiljana 8

Sesame Bar, accommodation and restaurant all rolled into one, they have live music on weekends. Fresh oysters from Ston are a speciality. Very intimate interior, but lots of outdoor seating on the upstairs terrace. ⓐ Dante Alighieria, five minutes west of Pile Gate

Talir If you happen to be in Dubrovnik during the summer festival, this is the place to meet actors and musicians who hang out here before or after performances. Check the walls: photos of Croatian celebrities adorn them. ⓐ On Antuninska

⬤ *The magic of Dubrovnik at dusk*

Korčula

This is the sixth-largest Adriatic island – and one of the greenest – with a good smattering of vineyards and olive groves. Because of the mild climate, there's a variety of vegetation from conifer forests and meadows of wildflowers to a typically Mediterranean coastline with coves and beaches. The walled town of Korčula, with all its historic associations, is why people mainly come to the island, but it's also interesting as a slice of traditional life. The population here is quite devout and the people observe many ancient religious ceremonies as well as keeping alive folk dances, songs, music and traditional costumes.

Korčula was first settled by the Greeks, but it wasn't until it was ruled by Venice that it became prosperous because of its flourishing shipbuilding industry. Stone was also quarried on the island by skilled local artisans and cut for export. Korčula's growth and expansion was brought to an end after a catastrophic outbreak of the plague in 1529, and the decline continued as Mediterranean trade diminished following the discovery of America. It wasn't until the early 20th century and the development of tourism that Korčula began to emerge from obscurity.

The main Rijeka-Dubrovnik ferry stops at the harbour of Korčula Town, along with other daily ferries making the run from Split to Vela Luka. By bus, there's a daily service from Dubrovnik that crosses the narrow stretch of water between the mainland and the island on a car ferry from Orebic. The bus station is 200 m southeast of the Old Town. **Tourist information office** (**t** 020 715 701 **w** www.korcula.hr) is on the western side of the peninsula.

Bikes are available for rental from outside the **Park Hotel**.

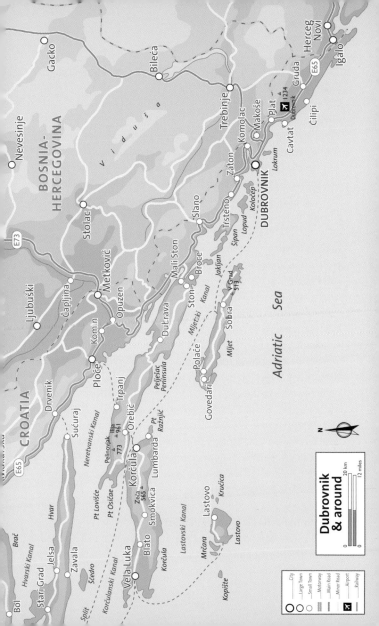

Dubrovnik
& around

SIGHTS & ATTRACTIONS

Beaches
While there are beaches in town, they're usually crowded and rocky, so the best bet is to take the bus to Lumbarda, about 8 km (5 miles) south of Korčula Town – the beaches are a 20-minute walk from the bus station but the great sand on **Prižna Bay** is worth it. **Bilin Žal**, just a short distance away, is rockier but has great views of the coastal mountains.

Korčula Town
From a bird's point-of-view, Korčula Town, the island's main settlement, looks like a fish on a platter with a central spine and ribs branching off on each side. This layout dates back to the 13th century, and was meant to reduce the effects of wind and sun. The town rises above its 13th-century walls like a mini-Dubrovnik. There is a distinct Venetian flavour to the architecture and culture – little wonder, because the Venetians took control of the island in the 10th century and stayed on for more than eight centuries. Most of the buildings date to the town's Golden Age (13th to 15th centuries) including one remaining town wall in the south; most of the others were demolished in the 19th century. The town has a special beauty, with its elegant 19th-century staircase sweeping up to **Kopnena Vrata** (Land Gate), the main entrance to the Old Town. This gate was completed in the 15th century along with the **Revelin**, the hulk of a defensive tower looming above it.

Crkva Sv Mihovila (St Michael's Church)
Standing just beyond the Land Gate, St Michael's Church is joined to a building by a small bridge that was used as a private entrance

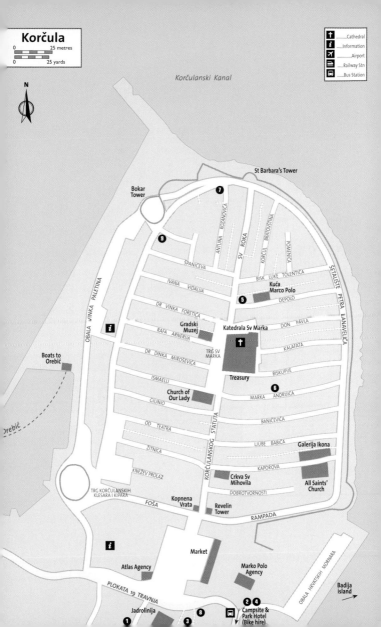

to the church by members of the medieval Brotherhood of St Michael.

Katedrala Sv Marka (St Mark's Cathedral)

This magnificent 15th-century limestone structure dominates Cathedral Square; it was built in the Gothic-Renaissance style by local and Italian workmen. It has an interesting portal decorated with a two-tailed mermaid, an elephant and other sculptures. On the façade, there's a beautiful fluted rose window and a

MARCO POLO LIVED HERE. PERHAPS.

Korčulans insist that their island was the birthplace of the famous explorer, despite a shortage of hard evidence, but then no other place seems to lay solid claims to Mr Polo. One firm bit of documentation says that Marco Polo was captured by the Genoese in a sea battle off Korčula in 1298; perhaps he was visiting relatives (there is a family long-resident on the island named de Polo). Korčulans insist, in any event, that Polo was born in 1254, went to Venice with his family in 1269, travelled the world and then, after being captured by the Genoese, was tossed into jail. It was during this period in jail that he wrote his famous book of adventures. What is certain is that he led an action-packed life, spending 17 years in China as a close personal friend of Kublai Khan. His famous travelogue sparked much interest in the Far East. Wherever he was born, the Korčulans are his biggest fans, and make a point of throwing celebrations to mark the key events in his life.

◀ *The magnificent portal of Katedrala Sv Marka*

strange cornice filled with even stranger beasts. Inside, look for the modern *Pièta* by famous sculptor Ivan Meštrović, and an altarpiece painting by Tintoretto. There's also a bronze statue of St Blaise by Meštrović.

Kuća Marco Polo (Marco Polo's House)

This is a 17th-century house that allegedly marks the spot where Marco Polo, adventurer, merchant and author of the world's first travel book, was born. The house was recently bought by the Korčula Town Authority, and plans are afoot to create a Museum of Marco Polo. For the time being, you can climb up to the tower-like upper storeys for a great view of the terracotta rooftops of the town.
ⓐ Kuća Marca Pola, in the alley Depolo ⓒ 10.00–13.00 & 17.00–19.00 June–Aug

Town walls and towers

The whole town is surrounded by robust 13th- to 15th-century walls and towers: there were a total of 12 in the Middle Ages. There are two principal entrances: **Kopnena Vrata** (Land Gate) and the Sea Gate on the west. The Revelin Tower, built by the Venetians in the 15th century, is topped with a terrace from which there are excellent views.

CULTURE

Galerija Ikona (Museum of Icons)

A permanent display of icons held by the All Saints' Brotherhood, including a haunting 15th-century triptych of the Passion as well as Byzantine icons painted on wood and some 17th- and 18th-century ritual objects. ⓐ Trg Svih Svetih ⓒ 10.00–12.00, 17.00–19.00 July & Aug

Gradski Muzej (Town Museum)

Housed in a Venetian palace located on the main square, the town museum stands just opposite the **cathedral**. The collection here includes historical items related to Korčula's history, including a copy of a 4th-century BC Greek tablet from Lumbarda, plus a room upstairs done up to show a typical Korčulan peasant kitchen.
ⓐ Pjaceta ⓛ 09.00–13.00, 17.00–19.00 July & Aug; 09.00–13.00 Mon–Sat rest of the year

RETAIL THERAPY

The main thing to take home from Korčula and the Pelješac Peninsula are foodstuffs, particularly the wines. Dingač is the most famous red wine and hard to find outside Croatia. The best plan is to go directly to the producer at wineries on the island. Olive oils are produced all through the country, but buying directly from the Korčulan grower seems to add a special quality to the oil.

TAKING A BREAK

Cukarin £ ❶   A sweet shop famous for its selection of home-baked biscuits and other delicious goodies. ⓐ in the narrow alley running south from Plokata 19 travnja

Fresh £ ❷   This restaurant is true to its name and produces fruit-filled smoothies, wraps and their touted Viva!Mex: ground beef, beans and homemade salsa. ⓐ 1 Kod Kina Liburne (between the bus station and the Old Town)
ⓣ 385 91 799 2086

Kiwi £ ❸ This is a good bet for a cool, soothing ice cream. ⓐ just off Plokata

Grubinjac ££ ❹ An old rustic farmhouse on the way from Korčula to Zmovo village, with great views over the hills beyond. Meals and snacks can be served on the terrace with the restaurant's home-produced wine. ⓐ Antae Skokandic Braco, Smovo ☎ 020 711 410

AFTER DARK

Restaurants

Konoba Adio Mare ££ ❺ This is on the vaulted ground floor of a house in Old Town next to Marco Polo's house. Patrons share long wooden tables and benches. Lots of atmosphere as Chef Cvijo jokes around while grilling lunch or dinner in front of your eyes. Seafood is excellent, and so is their bean and noodle soup. Or try the Korčulanska pasticada. Hard to get a table after 21.00, so reservations are a must. ⓐ Sv. Roka 2, Old Tow ☎ 020 711 253

Konoba Marinero ££ ❻ Offers homemade specialities and delicious grilled fish in a room filled with maritime bric-a-brac, or out on the terrace squeezed into a narrow alley. ⓐ Ulica Marka Andrijica 13 (just off Pjaceta main square) ☎ 020 711 170

Morski Konjić (The Sea Horse) ££ ❼ A cosy little restaurant at the northern tip of town, it is hung with fishing nets and serves a selection of meats and fish. (There is a more expensive Sea Horse restaurant on the eastern side of town.) ⓐ Šetwalište Petra Kanavelića ☎ 020 711 642

Planjak ££ ❽ An established and unpretentious place with a full range of grilled food, especially grilled kebabs. The restaurant has a shaded terrace. ⓐ Plokata 19 Travnja, in the centre of Old Town, just a few steps from the main ferry terminal ⓣ 020 71 1015

Kanavelic ££–£££ ❾ Specialises in very fresh fish and seafood including mussels washed down with the best local wines. (Try the octopus salad.) Considered formal dining – the grilled scampi are a speciality. ⓐ Sveta Barbara 12, near Hotel Korčula ⓣ 020 711 800

Bars & clubs
Nightlife in Korčula is limited to a couple of bars and whoever happens to be 'star billing' at the island's hotels to entertain guests. There is one good disco in town, **Disco Gaudi**, which seems to hit its stride around 02.00

Dos Locos A bar with lots of outdoor seating and a lively atmosphere. ⓐ Šetalište Frana Kršinića

Olea A favourite with young people, visitors and locals both. A friendly, sometimes boisterous atmosphere. ⓐ located between the bus station and Old Town on Prolaz tri sulara

ACCOMMODATION

Hotels & guesthouses
Badija £ Located on the island of Badija and reached by taxi-boat from the harbour, this is a restored monastery. Think 'austere' – but there's a beach and sports facilities. ⓐ Badija Island ⓣ 020 711 115

Bon Repos ££ On the road to Lambarda, this is a large hotel complex with pool and recently renovated comfortable rooms. ☎ 020 711 102

Korčula ££ This is the oldest of the town's hotels and was the town hall during Austrian times. The rooms are comfy if slightly frayed. @ Obala Dr. Franje Tudmana ☎ 020 711 078

Park ££ This hotel won't win any architectural awards, but there is a beach and many of the rooms have balconies. @ Šetalište Frana Kršinića ☎ 020 726 004

Apartments

With limited hotel accommodation, there are a number of private rooms and apartments available. It's best to deal with one of the agencies in town that do the booking for these: **Atlas**, @ Plokata 19 ☎ 020 711 060/711 231 @ atlas-korcula@du.htnet.hr; **Marko Polo**, @ Bilinc 5 ☎ 020 715 400 @ marko-polo-tours@du.tel.hr; **Turisticka Agencija Korčula**, @ just off Plokata 19 ☎ 020 711 067 @ htp-korcula@du.tel.hr

Camping

Camping Kalac is the nearest campsite (near the Bon Repos Hotel) – wooded with clean facilities. ☎ 020 711 115. Quieter choices would be **Palma** at the northern end of Luka Banja village (☎ 020 721 311) or **Oskorusica** in an olive grove ☎ 020 710 747

◐ *Green hills and blue seas frame the picturesque town of Korčula*

Cavtat

Sitting on a peninsula between two bays, Cavtat (pronounced tsavtat) lies about 16 km (10 miles) south of Dubrovnik and makes a good day trip or short visit. Even though Cavtat is popular with packaged tours, the hotel area is away from the village centre so the place still exudes a bit of charm. The seafront promenade is lined with bars, restaurants and palm trees, giving it a decidedly Mediterranean feel and about 1 km (½ mile) east of the town centre there's a *žal* or beach area.

Originally a colony founded by Greeks and known as Epidaurum, Cavtat went through the usual period of invasion and pillaging before establishing itself as a fishing village. It was rediscovered during the days of the Austro-Hungarian Empire at the beginning of the 20th century and became the playground of the rich.

Bus No 10 runs to Cavtat from Dubrovnik every hour, and there are a couple of ferry companies, with varying timetables, that serve the route. For people visiting Croatia by car, Cavtat is a good alternative to staying in Dubrovnik. The accommodation tends to be more reasonably priced and there are no parking problems.

SIGHTS & ATTRACTIONS

The town's best **beaches** lie to the east and west, about 1 km (½ mile) to the east where all the large package hotels are, and to the west in front of the Hotel Croatia. There are also pleasant walks around the headlands where you can swim off the rocks.

Cemeteries may not be on everyone's 'must-do' list but this is one that should be seen. Sitting on a beautiful hilltop overlooking the sea, the showpiece is the **Račić Mausoleum**, built by famous sculptor Ivan Meštrović for the daughter of a wealthy ship-owning family (it was rumoured that Meštrović was her lover). This white marble sepulchre was built in 1922 and is an eclectic mix of angels, eagles, dogs and so on. After the monument was completed, the entire family died in quick succession.

CULTURE

Formerly the home of Vlaho Bukovac, a talented painter born in Cavtat, **Galerija Bukovac** is now a gallery dedicated to his works. Bukovac studied in Paris and travelled widely through Europe before returning to Croatia and playing an important role in the development of Croatian art. His paintings – portraits as well as many other subjects – combine a photographic realism with touches of impressionism. Bukovac ended his career as a professor of fine arts in Prague.

The 16th-century **Rector's Palace** holds more of Vlaho Bukovac's work, along with drawings by Croatian and foreign artists, old coins, and a lapidarium with Roman stone pieces from the 1st century AD. It is also known as the Baltazar Bogisic Collection after a lawyer and cultural activist who spent his life promoting Croatian literature and learning.

AFTER DARK

Restaurants
Konoba Kolona £ A budget restaurant serving tasty fare. Shady terrace near the bus stop. ⓐ Put Od Tihe 2 ⓣ 020 478 269

Feral Restaurant ££ The Hotel Croatia (see below) has good food and live music every night. ① 020 475 555 ⓦ www.hoteli-croatia.hr

Konavoski Dvori ££–£££ For a grand meal out, this is a highly praised restaurant beside a working watermill on the River Ljuta about 18 km (11 miles) east of Cavtat. Waitresses are in the local Konavali costume and specialities of the house include lamb and trout. ⓐ Ljuta, Konavle

🔺 *Deliciously fresh fish is served everywhere in the region*

Leut ££–£££ Right in the centre of town, this restaurant has been around for three decades serving fresh and delicious seafood. An outdoor terrace is open in the summer months. ⓐ Trubićev Put 11 ⓣ 020 478 477

ACCOMMODATION

Private rooms and apartments Contact the Adriatica Agency, ⓐ A Thrumbicev Put 3 ⓣ 020 478 713 ⓔ adriatica@du.hinet.hr. Also ⓦ www.dubrovnik-online.com for more rooms and apartments

Albatros ££ This is one of the beachfront hotels that caters for package holiday guests. It has a private swimming pool and rooms have air-conditioning. ⓣ 020 479 833

Hotel Supetar ££ Right in the centre of town, on the harbour front, this is an older hotel that has been tastefully modernised. ⓐ Dr Ante Starčevića ⓣ 020 479 833 ⓦ www.hoteli-croatia.hr

Hotel Croatia £££ This is a huge, 482-room, 5-star hotel on the ridge of the Sustjepan peninsula. It offers all the amenities (TV, air-conditioning, swimming pool and private beaches, nudist and otherwise). ⓣ 020 475 555 ⓦ www.hoteli-croatia.hr

The Elaphite Islands

This string of 'car-less' islands, 14 in all (three of which are inhabited), lies between Dubrovnik and the Pelješac peninsula. They are considered one of Croatia's 'best-kept secrets'. What they offer is an area of rich vegetation, unspoiled nature (their name means 'deer') and a long architectural heritage. Dotted here and there are 15th- and 16th-century Gothic and Renaissance churches together with some pre-Romanesque chapels. Dubrovnik, with its shifting cultures, casts a strong influence over the Elaphites and their villages.

Ferries leave several times a day from Dubrovnik for the main Elaphite islands. Once there, visitors get around on foot, since cars are not allowed. For Lokrum there are boats leaving on the half-hour every day during high season and on weekends from the port in Dubrovnik's Old Town. Out of season, there are people with private boats who may take you across. Ask around.

SIGHTS & ATTRACTIONS

Koločep

Less than a half-hour away by ferry, this is the first of the inhabited Elaphite Isles and a very easy day trip. There are two small villages, **Donje Čelo** and **Gornje Celo**, on an island that is just over 2.6 sq km (1 sq mile) in area and that has a population of around 150 people.

The biggest attractions here are the **walks** through sweet-smelling pine and deciduous forests, with perhaps a picnic halfway through. In season (after May) there are a couple of restaurants on the waterfront where you can end the day eating freshly grilled seafood. The only accommodation on the island

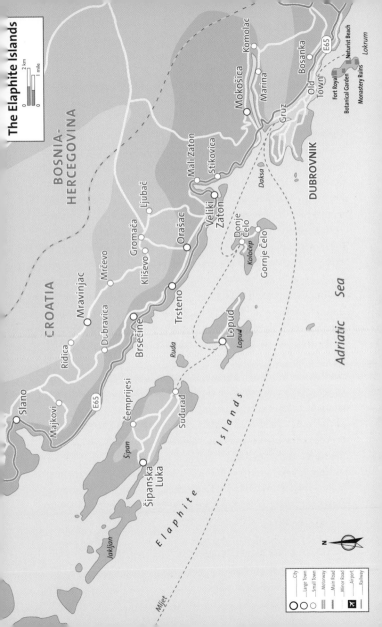

The Elaphite Islands

0 ___ 2 km
0 ___ 1 mile

BOSNIA-HERCEGOVINA

CROATIA

Slano
Majkovi
Ridica
Mravinjac
Dubravica
Mrčevo
Kliševo
Gromača
Ljubač
Mali Zaton
Stikovica
Orašac
Veliki Zaton
Brsečine
Trsteno
Čemprijesi
Suđurađ
Šipanska Luka
Šipan
Jakljan
Ruda
Lopud
Lopud
Donje Čelo
Koločep
Gornje Čelo
Daksa
Mljet

Mokošica
Komolac
Marina
Bosanka
Gruz
Old Town
Fort Royal
Botanical Garden
Monastery Ruins
Naturist Beach
Lokrum
DUBROVNIK

E65

Adriatic Sea

Elaphite Islands

N

City
Large Town
Small Town
Motorway
Main Road
Minor Road
Airport
Railway

is the **Villa Koločep**, a group of eight modern units above Donje Čelo beach. ☎ 020 757 025

Lokrum

Lokrum is a tiny island, just 2 km (1¼ mile) long. According to local legend, one of its earliest famous visitors came a trifle unwillingly. Richard the Lionheart, on his way home from the Crusades in 1192, encountered a fierce storm offshore. Like others facing shipwreck, he vowed that – if he was saved – he would build a church in thanks. He landed on Lokrum to fulfil his promise, but was persuaded that his money would be better spent if he built in Ragusa (Dubrovnik) rather than on an insignificant island.

Just 15 minutes by boat from the quay in Dubrovnik's Old Town, subtropical, uninhabited Lokrum is wonderfully undeveloped. Peace and tranquillity reign, and the biggest attractions are the **beaches** (cleaner and less crowded than Dubrovnik) and a network of **trails** that crisscross the island. Lokrum also has a protected naturist beach, one of the country's premier nudist beaches, on the southeastern end, and a warm, **saltwater lake**. The island has a great variety of flora including an old **Botanical Garden** with palms, cacti, vines, Australian eucalyptus, ancient trees and herbs running rampant. The garden was established in 1959 as an experiment to see if tropical plants would grow from seed and thrive in a Mediterranean climate.

Fort Royal is a fortress in the Lokrum hills, built in the shape of a star by the French in 1806. It's a steep, 20-minute hike up rickety steps, but from the top there are great views of Dubrovnik, Cavtat and the islands.

Lopud

Just beyond Koločep, Lopud was once a lively retreat for the noble families of Dubrovnik and remnants of their palatial houses can still be found. On the northern end of the island, the village of **Lopud** curves around a wide bay and a sandy beach.

Šipan, aka 'The Golden Island' is the largest of the Elaphites at 16.5 sq km (6½ sq miles), and yet the least developed. The main attraction here is the peace, quiet and gentle walks especially the 7-km (4¼-mile) walk from Suđurađ to Šipanska Luka on the island's northern end, which passes groves of figs, grapes and olives. There's a small sandy beach here and some good isolated spots for sunbathing, as well as a fine ruined villa on the harbour front.

CULTURE

The main relic of **Lopud**'s more vigorous past life is a fortified **Franciscan monastery** and **Crkva Gospe od Špilice (Church of Our Lady of the Rocks)** with its collection of altar paintings. The small **museum and treasury** at the end of the harbour has a series of 9th- to 11th-century frescoes in bad condition, some icons and other sacred objects and an assortment of other historic bits and pieces, from 500-year-old pudding bowls to 200-year-old French bayonets. Steps lead up to a ruined palace and private chapel built for Miho Pracat, a somewhat legendary 16th-century ship-owner and merchant who allegedly saved Spain from starvation and made himself a fortune at the same time. His bust stands in the Rector's Palace in Dubrovnik.

In **Šipan**, ruined villas are scattered all over the island, remnants of an era when Dubrovnik was powerful, along with ruined

churches going back many centuries. In **Suđurađ**, the ferry's first stop, there are the ruins of a summer palace built by a 16th-century ship-owner, and the **Church of the Holy Spirit**, built to guard locals from pirates.

ACCOMMODATION

There are no hotels or restaurants on Lokrum.

In Lopud, the tourist office (open May to mid-October) has a list of rooms for anyone wishing to stay longer than a day, and there are two hotels, the Lafodia (☎ 020 759 022) and Villa Vilina (☎ 020 759 333).

Private rooms are available on Šipan island for overnighters and there is a harbour-side hotel, the Šipan (☎ 020 758 000). There are a couple of bars and a restaurant in the hotel and absolutely no nightlife on the island.

▶ *Lopud was once a favoured retreat for noble families*

Mljet

Mljet, perhaps Dalmatia's most beautiful island, with its steep rocky cliffs, has remained almost untouched through the centuries and has a mystery or two. Even though Malta lays claim to the legend of Calypso and Ulysses and the visit of St Paul after a shipwreck, Mljet may be a more likely base for the stories. Once called Melita, it was infested with snakes until the 19th century and St Paul was supposedly bitten by one (Malta has no snakes). The mongoose was imported to Mljet to control the snake. The mongooses flourished and multiplied, thereby curing the snake problem but causing a mongoose problem in the process. The island's vast **National Park**, which occupies the entire western end of the island, is what mainly draws visitors to Mljet. It can be done in a day trip. A single road runs the length of the island.

The crossing from Dubrovnik takes four hours on the daily Jadrolinija ferry and in the summer one-and-a-half hours on the fast catamaran that leaves Dubrovnik in the morning and returns in the afternoon. The ferries dock just to the east of **Sobra** and there are buses that take you into town, but there can be a problem in the summer when there are more passengers than buses. For day-trippers, the catamaran will dock at **Polače**. To get away from transportation headaches, the best idea is to book an all-inclusive package deal from one of the travel agencies; these include ferry, a tour, a chance to swim and a trip out to the island on the lake.

Aside from the buses that meet the ferries, there's no local transport. However, you can hire bikes, cars or scooters from several outlets, the biggest of which is the **Hotel Odisej** in Pomena. For more information on Mljet contact the tourist office in Polače.
☏ 020 744 125

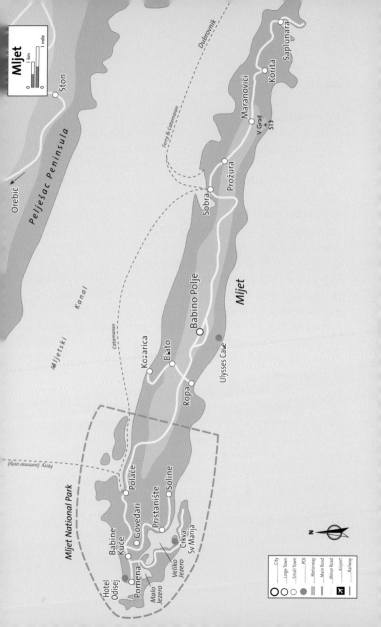

SIGHTS & ATTRACTIONS

Mljet National Park

This is a Croatian national treasure and beside the peace, quiet and lack of commercial development is the main attraction on the island. Since it was never ruled by Venice, no trees were chopped down to build major towns, so the pine and oak forest with its two saltwater lakes has remained unspoiled. The larger of these two lakes, **Veliko Jezero** (Big Lake), has an island with a charming but run-down 12th-century monastery that still displays bits of its Romanesque and Renaissance architecture. The monastery was a hotel in its last incarnation but, since being returned to the Benedictines, restoration has begun and there are Sunday services in the church. You can visit the monastery gardens when they are open and there is a restaurant on the island where lunch is served. The island also has a ten-minute walk where you can gather wild asparagus in the summer or visit two simple chapels built by sailors. There are boats in Pristanište that shuttle visitors back and forth to the island several times a day, with the fee included in the national park entry. A network of paths crisscross the park for walking or mountain biking, and there's a 9-km (5½-mile) trail that runs around the perimeter of the lakes. For a great view of the Pelješac Peninsula and the island of Korčula, there's a steep path up to the highest point in the park, **Montokuc**. ⓦ www.np-mljet.hr

Polače

The main attraction of this harbour town are the remains of a 1st to 4th-century Roman palace with fortifications that lie just above the town, and the ruins of an ancient Christian basilica in a sheltered bay.

Saplunara

This stunning sand beach below a small village of the same name is a great day trip or two-or three-day getaway, if you can find accommodation. Families let rooms during the season and there are a couple of basic fish restaurants – and for total relaxation, you can get rid of clothes at a long, deserted, sandy nudist beach that is a 20-minute walk from Saplunara.

Ulysses cave

According to legend, Ulysses stayed here for seven years during his epic voyage. Whether this is true or not, there is a cave directly south of **Babino Polje** that can be explored by boat (the easiest way) or by trekking across the fields for a half-hour or so and climbing down to the cave (Odisejeva spilja).

A DIVER'S PARADISE.

Jacques Cousteau praised the Adriatic Coast as one of the world's greatest dive locations and for good reason: the coastal waters are crystal clear and hold some very good dive attractions. One of these is an ancient Roman vessel where little remains but some amphorae; a more modern location is a German U-boat. Divers must pay an initial fee of 100 Kn at one of the registered dive centres or at the local harbourmaster's office before they can dive. For novices, there are an increasing number of dive shops opening up all along the Adriatic coast, offering lessons, equipment rental and guided trips. Around Mljet, diving is restricted to organised groups. For more information on diving, contact the Croatian Diving Federation ⓐ Dalmatinska 12, 10000 Zagreb ⓦ www.diving.hr ⓦ www.diving-hrs.hr

TAKING A BREAK

In Pomena, a favourite docking site for yachtsmen, there are a string of small restaurants along the harbour and in Polače there are a couple of small restaurants, a provisions store that is open in the mornings and a bakery. The restaurant at the monastery also serves good lunches.

ACCOMMODATION

Hotel Odisej ££ in Pomena is a modern 3-star hotel that is open from Easter until November. It has 150 rooms, some with a balcony and sea view. The hotel lies in the national park and is a 15-minute walk from Malo Jezero, so it's a good base for a hiking holiday. ℹ 020 744 022 ⓦ www.hotelodisej.hr

Private rooms and campsites that are clean and comfortable are available in Pomena and Polače at reasonable prices, but these should be booked in advance. The tourist office in Polače can supply the names of people who will rent rooms. ℹ 020 745 125. For booking ahead, Mini Brum tourist agency in Babino Polje can be reached at ℹ 020 285 566. There are also campsites in Babino Polje and in Ropa and a few run by private individuals. Ask a local for more information.

▶ *The island of Mljet is beautiful and unspoilt*

Pelješac Peninsula

This is one of those places that people can often pass straight through without knowing what they're missing. Geographically (see map on page 99), it's a long, narrow peninsula – it's 62 km (39 miles) long but is never more than 7 km (4½ miles) wide. It feels like an island, though, and there's the sense of always being near water. Isolated and undeveloped, Pelješac is mainly known for its two excellent wines (Postup and Dingač) both of which can be tasted in cellars that are open to the public in the summer. Ragusa (Dubrovnik) owned the peninsula from the 12th to the early 19th century, and many of the Republic's finest seafarers came from this region.

Buses from Dubrovnik bound for Korčula make stops at Ston and Orebić three times a day, but to really explore the peninsula properly, a rental car is recommended.

SIGHTS & ATTRACTIONS

Orebić

With its history as a trade centre for 500 years, Orebić has a colourful seafaring past and was once quite prosperous, earning money from building ships to supply a merchant fleet. Today it's a centre for tourism mainly because of its beaches, excellent climate and its proximity to a number of hiking trails. There are some attractions, like the 15th-century **Franjevački Samostan** (Franciscan Monastery) that is located about a 20-minute walk out of town, with its famous (and allegedly miraculous) icon, Gospa od Angela (Our Lady of the Angels). It was believed the icon would protect mariners from shipwreck, and there are numerous votive offerings from sailors and sea captains who believe it was the Lady who saved their lives. There is also a Virgin and Child by Nikola Firentinac, the 15th-century Renaissance master, who also designed the dome at Šibenik Cathedral.

There's a great view of the Pelješac channel from the monastery terrace.

Ston

This fortified town has a split personality: **Mali Ston** is on the north coast and **Veliki Ston** on the south coast. The most impressive feature in Veliki Ston (sometimes called simply Ston) are 14th-century walls that were built to defend Dubrovnik's northern borders. These stretch for 3 km (1¾ miles) across a rugged hillside. Ston doesn't look like much at first glance because rebuilding has been slow since the 1996 earthquake, but this small village attracts visitors and people from Dubrovnik en route to Korčula. They come to eat the fresh, succulent oysters produced in Mali Ston Bay that are prepared in a dozen and one ways, from raw and slippery to baked in delicate sauces. While oysters take top billing, restaurants feature ultra-fresh fish dinners as well.

Historically, Ston's major importance was as a salt-producer: when Napoleon invaded Dubrovnik he was as keen to get control of Ston's salt as he was to occupy Dubrovnik. Twenty of the original 40 towers along the fortifying walls – and 5 km (3 miles) of the walls themselves – are still standing, and from the top you can get great views of Mljet. There are some interesting Gothic and Renaissances houses here too.

About a 15-minute walk away is Mali Ston. It doesn't have a beach, but you can swim in the clear water from the jetty or rocks. To the north there's a ruined fortress with steps leading to a parapet and great views.

AFTER DARK

Restaurants

Restaurant Mlinica ££ is on the ground floor of the Ostrea hotel.
☏ 020 754 555 **Ⓦ** www.ostrea.hr

Kapetanova Kuca ££–£££ On the waterfront of Mali Ston, this was once the residence of a captain of the guards. Good seafood menu and a wide selection of wines. **☏** 020 754 555 **Ⓦ** www.ostrea.hr

Vila Koruna ££–£££ Both a hotel and a splendid restaurant right on the water. It serves oysters and seafood freshly chosen from stone tanks that sit under the plate-glass windows on the covered terrace of the restaurant. The owner is very friendly, and a simple meal can easily turn into an evening party with dancing. It's the oldest eating spot in the region, with oysters, mussels and lobster as its speciality.
ⓐ Mali Ston **☏** 020 754 999 **ⓔ** vila-koruna@du.t-com.hr
Ⓦ www.vilakoruna.cjb.net

Nightlife

There's not usually much evening entertainment during the week – aside from the local colour at the hotels and restaurants – but Veliki Ston has concerts and other festivities on weekends. Check with the tourist bureau to find out what's on the agenda.

ACCOMMODATION

Hotel Bellevue ££ The hotel sits in a pine wood just 20 metres from a pebble beach and has a pool, restaurant and pizzeria. **ⓐ** Sv.Križ 103, Orebić **☏** 020 713 148/022 **Ⓦ** www.orebic-htp.hr

Hotel Orsan ££ A 3-star hotel surrounded by pine and cypress trees on a quiet, sandy bay just a short distance from the sea. ⓐ Bana Jelačića 119 ⓣ 020 713 026 ⓦ www.orebic-htp.hr

Ostrea ££ Classed as a family-owned 3-star, but the nine rooms offered are more upmarket than others on the Peninsula – even including a 'presidential suite'. The hotel also has two good restaurants with a mouth-watering selection of seafood from starters to main (check out the menu on the web). ⓐ Mali Ston ⓣ 020 754 555 ⓦ www.ostrea.hr

Fresh oysters are a local speciality

● *Excellent wines are produced on the peninsula*

▶ *Detail of stonework on the Diocletian Palace, Split*

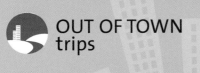

Split

Split is a place that oozes atmosphere: little wonder, given that this major city actually grew out of a Roman emperor's palatial retirement home. Begun in 295 AD, it took Emperor Diocletian ten years to build. The 'court' included living quarters for courtiers, a garrison to guard them, and soldiers to man the garrison. In total the fortified site measured 4,500 sq m (48,438 sq ft); the luxurious apartments of the palace were surrounded by lush gardens. After Diocletian died and left his mini-empire, a succession of despots gradually ran the palace into the ground over the next couple of centuries, until refugees fleeing barbarian invasions moved in and began to restore it.

Modern Split is the second biggest city in Croatia, with some 220,000 inhabitants and tourism as its major industry. Many of these tourists come for the **carnival** season, when masked revellers take over the streets for the **Feast of St Domnius** in May. St Domnius is the city's protector (and patron saint of woodworkers), so the markets are full of craftsmen selling their wares during feast days. Split is a lively and friendly city; although it was not bombarded during the 1991 war, it did suffer from the huge influx of refugees and there was a big drop in tourism.

Nowadays the visitors have returned. **Tourist information** has an office adjacent to the cathedral on the Peristil and here you can find maps of the city, ferry schedules and current phone numbers and addresses for local attractions, eating places, accommodation, and so on. The office also sells the Split Card that permits free entry or a discount for museums and galleries plus discounts on car hire, hotels and restaurants. ❶ 020 347 100 ⓦ www.visitsplit.com ⓛ 08.00–20.00 Mon–Fri, 08.00–13.00 Sat, 09.00–13.00 Sun

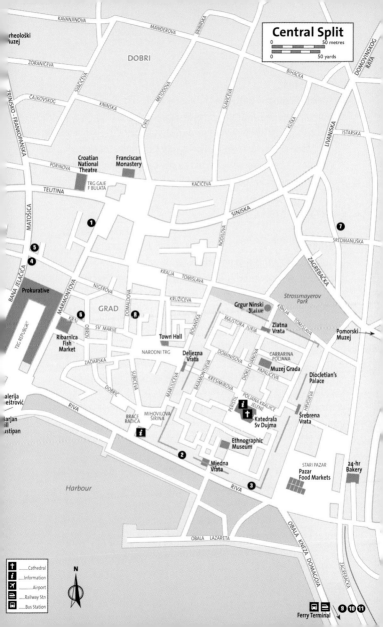

Getting there

Airlines fly regularly between Dubrovnik and Split.
ⓦ www.croatiaairlines.hr. There are frequent buses from Dubrovnik;
the journey takes about 4.5 hours and should be booked in advance.
There is also a regular train service ⓦ www.hznet.hr; both train and
bus stations are just southeast of the city centre. In the summer there
are ferry connections between Korčula, Hvar (Stari Grad) and Split.

SIGHTS & ATTRACTIONS

Beaches

Locals usually journey out to the islands when they want to swim
and enjoy the sunshine, but the main city beach at **Bačviće** is clean
and you can rent a sunbed and an umbrella there. There are also
toilets, showers and bars near the beach. At **Bene**, on the **Marjan
Peninsula**, there are some rocky coves and shady spots, plus showers
and a refreshment bar.

Diocletian's Palace

For visitors, the main attraction is the Old Town, encircled by town
walls with **Diocletian's Roman palace** at its heart. It's hard to get an
image of what the palace must have looked like in the 4th century,
since so much of it has been built around and incorporated into the
Old Town centre. Little remains of the imperial apartments,
although the medieval structures that took their place were built
of the stone used in the palace. What used to be Diocletian's
mausoleum now stands as **Katedrala Sv Dujma** (Cathedral of
St Domnius), and the baptistery was once a temple. During the
period between World War I and World War II, this whole area
was badly run down and filled with émigrés and red-light bars –

today, it's once again the centre of things, with lots of shops and tourists.

For anyone interested in Roman structures, there are maps available of the original palace and lots of detailed information on the temple, the cathedral, the underground chambers, the peristyle and the many altars. You can enter the area via one of four gates: **Zlatna Vrata** (Golden Gate), **Deljezna Vrata** (Iron Gate), **Šrebrena Vrata** (Silver Gate) and **Mjedna Vrata** (Bronze Gate).

Marjan

This nature reserve is located on a compact 3.5-km (2¼-mile) peninsula and is planted with a green assortment of Aleppo pines, cypresses, rosemary and holm oak. Nearby the ample terrace of the Vidilica Café has panoramic views of Split From Vidilica, there's a path along the south side of Marjan that leads to the 13th-century Romanesque church of **Sv Nikola** and the 15th-century church of **Sv Jere**, built on the remains of an ancient temple.

Pazar and Ribarnica (food markets)

This colourful open-air fruit and vegetable market (Pazar) stands just outside the palace walls and is open every day. Since the people of Split haven't totally succumbed to supermarkets, this is where they shop for fresh produce. Photographers love the market and its wildly colourful assortment of peppers, tomatoes, melons, grapes, pomegranates and other delicacies. The Ribarnica (covered fish market) is nearby.

ⓐ just east of Peristil, the Šrebrena Vrata leads onto Pazar
ⓒ 07.00–13.00 Mon–Sat, 07.00–11.00 Sun.

Sustipan

For quiet walks, the cypress gardens of Sustipan have wonderful views to the sea and Split plus some park benches on which to rest, to exchange news or to meditate. You can see the foundations of an early medieval church called **Sv Stipe** (St Stephen) here in the remains of a Benedictine monastery. In the centre of the gardens stands a 19th-century neoclassical pavilion.

CULTURE

Arheološki Muzej (Archeological Museum)

Founded in 1820, this is a well-displayed collection of Roman, Illyrian, Greek and medieval artefacts that includes jewellery, amulets,

● *The skyline of Split boasts a dynamic mix of ancient and new*

ceramics, glassware and coins. (Don't miss the lewd oil lamp!) Outside, in an arcaded courtyard and garden, there are pieces of decorative sculpture, sarcophagi and early Christian stelae.

ⓐ Zrinjsko-Frankopanska 25 ⓣ 020 318 714 ⓛ 09.00–14.00 Tues–Sun

Pomorski Muzej (Maritime Museum)

Divided into two sections – naval war and naval trading – this museum is intriguing even for non-sailors. There are model ships done to scale, naval paintings, and lots of sailing equipment. Of special interest are the world's first self-propelled torpedoes. Designed by Ivan Blaz Lupis, a Croat, and developed in conjunction with the British engineer Robert Whitehead, the model was successfully trialled in 1866.

ⓐ Glagoljaška 18 ⓣ 020 347 346 ⓛ 09.00–13.30, 18.00–21.00 Tues–Sun

DIOCLETIAN, THE EGOMANIACAL EMPEROR

The Emperor Diocletian enjoyed pursuing grandiose plans and had a limitless passion for building; his constructions included basilicas, circuses, a mint, an arms factory and lots of grand houses for his relatives. Another of his major projects were the **Terme di Diocleziano**, the Diocletian Baths, a bathing establishment that was meant to outshine Rome's largest and most luxurious bath. Over a period of five years starting in 300 AD, more than 10,000 Christian prisoners were used as forced labour to construct the massive edifice that was to accommodate 3,000 bathers with hot, cold and steam baths plus dressing rooms, gyms, meeting rooms, libraries and gardens. Marble facades graced the exterior and inside mosaic floors were part of a structure covering 13 hectares.

The emperor was born as the son of slaves in Dalmatia, possibly growing up in Salona. He rose up through the ranks in the Roman military and became emperor in 284 AD at the age of 39. Among his positive achievements were that he brought some stability and direction to a Roman Empire already under pressure from barbarian incursions. In an attempt to ensure the continuation of the Empire, he created a system of parcelling out authority for the Empire, dividing it into four regions, each separately ruled by an emperor. The power-sharing system soon disintegrated once he 'retired', however, and in fact led to his family's downfall. On the less savoury side, Diocletian is also remembered for his ruthless persecution of Christians: many of the country's saints were martyred at his command.

Galerija Meštrović (Meštrović Gallery)

This monumental villa, built in the early 1930s, was chosen by Ivan Meštrović, the famous Croatian sculptor, as a summer residence and studio. He lived here until he fled the country during World War II. There are almost 200 sculptures on display, both inside the villa and outside in the gardens, in wood, marble, stone and bronze, and dating from the beginning of the century to 1946.

ⓐ Šetalište Ivana Meštrovića 46 ☎ 020 358 450 🕒 09.00–21.00 Tues–Sun, mid-May–end Sept; 09.00–16.00 Tues–Sat, 10.00–15.00 Sun, winter

🔺 The Meštrović Gallery houses works by the famed sculptor

RETAIL THERAPY

Arts, crafts and antiques

For those who like antique shops, **Antikvarnica** (ⓐ Cosmija 1, near Sarajevo Restaurant) and **Anatik Shop & Galerija** (ⓐ Trg Cararina Poliana), are worth some browsing time. For handicrafts, the market in the cellars of Diocletian's Palace has a good assortment.

Foodstuffs

For high quality Croatian wines, honey, olive oils and truffles, check out the **Vinoteka sv. Martin** (ⓐ Majstora Jurja 17). More Croatian wines are found at **Vinoteka Bouquet** (ⓐ Riva 3, west of Trg Republike). For plain, everyday food of great quality such as *rakija*, buns and cakes and wine, it is best to go to the **market** east of **Šrebrena Vrata** (Silver Gate).

TAKING A BREAK

For picnics and snacks on the hoof, the best place to head is the daily market at the eastern edge of the Old Town, where you can pick up the ingredients for a picnic – hams, cheeses, tomatoes, lettuce, olives, etc. If you need a bigger range of goods, the **Gavrilović** supermarket is open from 07.00 to 23.00. ⓐ Obala kneza Domagoja, at the ferry terminal.

The 24-hour bakery **Prerada** intoxicates with its freshly baked breads, cakes and strudels. ⓐ On Zagrebacka opposite the market.

◖ *Croatia boasts more than 2,000 km (1,250 miles) of spectacular coastline*

Babić £ ❶ This is a good place for a takeaway pizza slice, the omnipresent and delicious *pršut*, sandwiches and pastries.
ⓐ Marmontova 7

Bobis £ ❷ For those with a sweet tooth, Bobis has a large café on the Riva strip and a smaller outlet on Marmontova.

Ivona £ ❸ Croatian ice cream can be found in many outlets but some of the best is here. ⓐ Riva 25

Kantun Paulina £ ❹ This is the place to get *ćevapčići*, a kind of spicy meat rissole beloved by the Croatians for snack food.
ⓐ opposite Pizzeria Galija

AFTER DARK

Restaurants
Considering it's a tourist town, there's a curious shortage of high-quality restaurants in Old Town, but there are a few outside the city walls. A good area to check out is on the western edge of the Old Town in the lanes west of Trg Republike. Restaurants tend to stay open until 23.00 or midnight.

Pizzeria Galija £ ❺ Excellent pizza cooked in a charcoal oven plus lots of pasta and antipasti. ⓐ Tončićeva 12, a block north of Trg Republike ❶ 020 347 932

Zlatna Ribica £ ❻ A stand-up buffet with cheap seafood snacks that are chalked onto a blackboard. ⓐ Kraj svete Marije 12, right by the fish market ❶ 21.00 weekdays, 02.00 weekends

Konoba kod Jože ££ ❼ This cosy and intimate restaurant with fish nets on the wall is considered one of the best seafood restaurants in Split. Its risottos and pastas are a good bet and inexpensive. ⓐ Sredmanuška 4 (heading north through Strossmayerov Park this street is on the right) ❶ 020 347 397

Sarajevo ££ ❽ Right in the centre of the city, Sarajevo has Croatian meat and fish dishes. Try the *pasticada* (beef stuffed with lard, roasted in wine and spices). ⓐ Domaldova 6 ❶ 020 347 454

Stellon ££ ❾ In a country whose restaurants do mainly fish and meat, Stellon is a good bet for vegetarians with its hearty salads and pasta and veggie mains. Smart, slick, hyper-modern interior but reasonably priced. ⓐ Bačviće

Boban £££ ❿ For a gourmet meal, this is the number one choice – as it was for such luminaries as Placido Domingo. Croatian dishes are given an Italian twist in a nod to fusion cuisine with lobster done up as a spicy tomato stew and a fish carpaccio done sushi-style. Great wine list. ⓐ Hektoroviceva 49, parallel to Bačviće beach road Put Firula ❶ 020 543 300

Šumica £££ ⓫ The emphasis here is on presenting the freshest possible fish and shellfish, but there are other choices on the menu such as a sophisticated version of the omnipresent schnitzel. The 'smart set' hang out in this classy restaurant with its big outdoor terrace. ⓐ Put Firla 6 ❶ 020 389 897

Bars, clubs & discos

For what's playing, check the town website (Ⓦ www.visit-split.com), tourist information, the newspaper *Slobodna Dalmacija* or municipal posters displayed on billboards throughout the Old Town. These will also announce numerous open-air pop concerts that are held during the summer months, often at the Prokurative and the inner courtyard of Tvrdava Gripe. The wild nightlife scene in Split is not wild, especially in the summer, when a lot of people leave town for the islands.

Capo This is a café-bar at ground level that features a regular programme of rock, blues and cover bands three or four times a week. A 15-minute walk from the Old Town. Ⓐ At the Bačvice beach pavilion

Ghetto Club Tables pepper an outdoor courtyard in the summer – there are occasional exhibitions and performances for the alternative crowd. Ⓐ Dosud 10

Kanavelić For the 16–25 year old age group, this is considered the 'in' place to be. Lots of techno music that spills out onto a crowded outdoor terrace in the summer. Ⓐ Buvinina 1, opposite Prenošiste Slavija

Kocka An alternative club with a mixed programme of films, DJ nights and live gigs. Ⓐ a 15-minute walk northeast of the Old Town just off Slobode Ⓦ www.kocka.hr

Metropolis This mainstream disco has been around for a while and features a mix of commercial, techno and rock with occasional live concerts. ⓐ Matice Hrvatska 1 ⓣ 020 305 110

Tribu A big favourite with the young crowd located on the main city beach, north of the centre near the Poljud stadium. ⓐ Osmih Mediteranskih igara 3

Music and folk dancing Informal concerts featuring *klapa* singers (the Dalmatian male choirs) and other folk events are often held at lunchtime in either Nadroni trg or Peristil during the summer months. The tourist information office will have particulars.

ACCOMMODATION

Jupiter £ More or less a cross between a hotel and a hostel, the Jupiter has double, triple and quad rooms with shared bathrooms in the hallway. Good location and friendly. ⓐ Gravovceva sirina 1 ⓣ 020 344 801

Adriana ££ Small, very conveniently located hotel with modern double rooms right above the seafront café-pizzeria of the same name. Very comfortable and in high demand. ⓐ Riva 8 ⓣ 020 340 000 ⓦ www.hotel-adriana.hr

Bellevue Hotel Central ££ Overlooking the sea and comfortable and convenient if not stylish. ⓐ Bana Jelačića 2 ⓣ 020 345 644

Consul ££ On a quiet street about 1.5 km (1 mile) from Old Town with modern, comfortable rooms and a summer terrace. ⓐ Trscanska 34 ⓣ 020 340 130 ⓦ www.hotel-consul.net

Hotel Marjan ££ A building that's been around for a long time, but the rooms are still comfortable and well-equipped. Friendly staff. ⓐ Obala Kneza Branimira 8 ⓣ 020 399 211 ⓦ www.hotel-marjan.com

Hotel President £££ Lots of facilities with both plush rooms and apartments, this 4-star property is a five-minute walk north of the Old Town. ⓐ Starčevića 1 ⓣ 385 21 305 222 ⓦ www.hotelpresident.hr

Park £££ A fairly recently renovated hotel that has an exclusive feel to it and smartly decorated rooms. Good quality restaurant with an international menu. ⓐ Hatzeov pcrivoj 3 ⓣ 020 406 400

● *Diocletian's magnificent palace lies at the heart of Split*

Hvar

This is one of the most beautiful and popular offshore islands in Croatia, so it attracts tour groups from all over Europe. The capital, **Hvar Town**, has a 16th-century Venetian air, there are excellent beaches and the weather (according to fans) is sunnier and warmer than elsewhere. Locals insist there are 2,700 hours of sunshine and snow is rare. The main crop on the island is lavender and it's on sale everywhere – come in the spring and the air is heady with the scent. Wine is also produced, along with figs and olives.

Hvar Town, with its well-preserved Venetian Renaissance architecture, easily challenges Korčula and Dubrovnik in beauty, although the summer crowds can be a bit much. It's better to visit in the spring or autumn. The town wraps itself around a bay (**Luca Hvar**) and the main square, **Trg Sveti Stjepana**, which is allegedly the biggest main square in Dalmatia. Beyond the town, stone houses clamber up three hills to a peak crowned by a Venetian fortress. After Dubrovnik, this is probably the most fashionable of Adriatic resorts for Croats who love to sit in the cafés of the main square. ⓦ www.hvar.hr

GETTING THERE

The best travel links are to Split, with regular ferry connections from Stari Grad. A daily catamaran service also stops at Hvar Town on its way to and from the island of Lastovo to Split (Jadrolinija ⓣ 741 132). From Dubrovnik it is easiest to hire a car and cross on the ferry that runs from the mainland at Drvenik to Sućuraj on the eastern tip of the island. There are also links to Korčula in the south and thence to Dubrovnik.

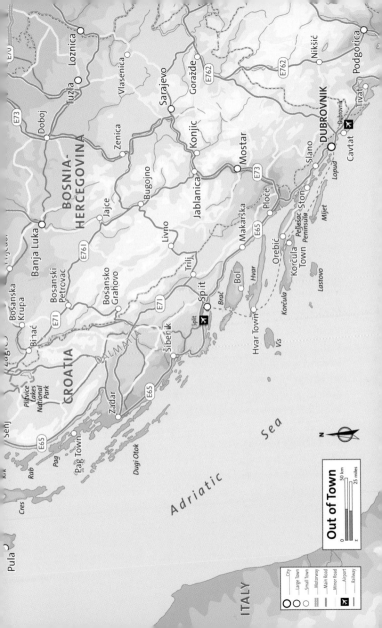

SIGHTS & ATTRACTIONS

Arsenal

This hulking 17th-century arcaded building dominates the square.
It was where war galleys were once hauled out to be repaired.
In 1612, the upper floor was converted into a theatre; it is the oldest
in Croatia and one of the first in Europe. Check out the inscription
inside – *Anno Secundo Pacis MDCXII*: this refers to the peace after
a century-long quarrel between commoners and aristocrats.
It followed an uprising in 1510 when 19 men were hanged from
galley masts. The theatre was built to calm the distrust between
nobles and commoners, since both classes shared theatrical space.
ⓐ Trg Sveti Stjepana

Benedictine Convent

This is small as convents go, but the tiny group of nuns here spend
their time making the extraordinary Hvar lace, which you see being
sold in shops in Hvar Town. The nuns never leave the grounds and
are bound by an oath of silence.
ⓐ Northwest of Trg Sveti Stjepana ⓣ 020 741 052
ⓛ 10.00–13.00, 16.00–18.00 July & Aug, Christmas & Holy Week

The Bishop's Treasury

Next door to the cathedral, this holds a small collection of
reliquaries, embroidery and chalices.
ⓐ Riznica ⓣ 020 741 269 ⓛ 09.00–12.00, 17.00–19.00 July & Aug,
Christmas & Holy Week

Citadel

Built in the 1550s by the Venetians (aided by Spanish engineers), the building is called Španjola locally. Inside, there's a marine archaeology collection and a display of amphorae and Greco-Roman drinking vessels. The biggest attraction is the view from the ramparts.

Hektorovič Palace

On the north side of the main square, this is a slightly spooky house that was left unfinished when it was built in the 15th century. Named after a famous poet, it has Venetian-Gothic windows, and is one of the best examples of Venetian architecture on the island.
🕐 Northwest of Trg Sveti Stjepana

Katedrala Sv Stjepana (St Stephen's Cathedral)

As a backdrop to the main square, this basilica was built between the 16th and 17th centuries on the foundations of an earlier monastery. It has a Renaissance trefoil facade and a lovely campanile; inside you can admire the 13th-century Madonna and child.
🕐 Trg Sveti Stjepana

Trg Sv Stjepana (St Stephen's Square)

Dating back to the 13th century, this imposing square opens onto the Mandrac, an enclosed harbour for small boats that leads to a larger bay. The old buildings lining the square have been converted into restaurants, galleries and small cafés.

AFTER DARK

Restaurants

There's a full range of eating places in Hvar. Grilled fish and meat and black risotto are on offer, as ever, but local specialities include Dalmatian stewed beef, fritters, fig torte and octopus salad.

Bacchus £ Open all year, popular with the locals, and the best place in town to get a reasonably priced steak. ⓐ Trg Sv Stejpana ⓣ 020 742 251

Bounty £–££ Reasonably priced grilled fish and meat with the mandatory seafood risottos. Try the excellent fish soup here washed down with the white house wine. ⓐ Fabrika, on the inner harbour.

Macondo ££–£££ A first-class fish restaurant with faultless food and service – but be prepared to wait for a table. It boasts a small terrace for summer dining and a large open fire for colder nights. ⓐ Groda, in a narrow alley between the main square and the fortress ⓣ 020 742 850

Pape ££–£££ The best thing about this restaurant is the view from the terrace; it is perched high above the harbour. But the fish and seafood are tasty. You can also sample some Balkan specialities here such as *muckalica* (a spicy paprika and pepper stew). ⓛ Ulica Pučkog Ustanka ⓣ 020 742 309

Bars
Carpe Diem Trendy cocktail bar that attracts all the 'beautiful people'. It overlooks the sea and has oriental wicker furniture and a plant-filled terrace. ⓐ Obala Oslobođenja ⓣ 020 742 369 ⓛ closes at 03.00 ⓦ www.carpe-diem-hvar.com

Cofein On the main square, there are tables outside almost all year long. ⓐ Trg Sv Stejepana

---

ⓞ *The Pakleni Islands lie off the coast of Hvar*

Jazz Walk south from the main square through the jumble of streets to find this laid-back bar with its fish-themed décor.

Loco On the main square, this is the best of the youth-oriented bars in town. Stylish, relaxing and chic. ⓐ Trg svetog Stjepana

ACCOMMODATION

To encourage visitors in the winter months, hotels advertise that they will give free board and lodging if the temperatures go below freezing during the day, and 50 per cent off if it rains for more than three hours during the day.

Whether travelling in the summer or the winter, it's a good idea to book rooms on Hvar well in advance. (See ⓦ www.suncanihvr.hr for additional hotel information.)

Dalmacija £ A basic but comfortable 2-star hotel on the seafront, a five-minute walk from the centre. ⓐ Obala Ivana Lučića-Lavčevića ⓣ 020 741 120

Podstine ££ This is a quiet, family-run hotel near a pebble beach about 20 minutes west of the main square. Seventeen rooms, each with a sea view and a lovely terrace restaurant. ⓐ Pod Stine ❶ 020 741 118

Slavia Hotel ££ A 3-star, three-storey hotel with ensuite rooms near the ferry dock. Breakfast is served on a terrace right by the harbour. ⓐ Obala oslobodenja ❶ 020 741 820

Palace Hotel £££ This 76-room 'palace', built during the Hapsburg era, sits on the edge of the main square overlooking the harbour. Amenities include an indoor heated swimming pool, massage and sauna. ⓐ Trg svetog Stjepana ❶ 020 741 966

🔻 *Lavender is the main crop on Hvar*

Pag

In any island beauty contest, Pag wouldn't even be a contender, but it does have qualities that make it well worth visiting. The island lies in the south of the Kvarner Gulf and is a stark and desolate place that looks like it couldn't possibly support any form of life. A small population (and three times as many sheep) do live there, however, and they produce two things that have made the islanders famous throughout Croatia – cheese and lace. Pag cheese is a hard, piquant sheep's cheese known as *paški sir* that tastes like a cross between old cheddar and parmesan. Its distinctive taste comes from a mixture of olive oil and ash that is rubbed into the cheese before it's left to mature and from the wild herbs (like sage) and the salty vegetation that the sheep eat. The cheese tends to be a bit

PAG LACE

This – along with salt making – is Pag's most famous industry, and a craft that remains very traditional and non-commercial. Once prized by emperors as 'white gold', the lace was only dubbed 'Pag lace' this century and a school established in the town. The work is painstaking and created using an ordinary darning needle; each piece is unique and done without a draft or plan. When it is finished it is firm, as if starched, and will stay that way even after washing. While you can buy Pag lace in shops in Dubrovnik, it's a special experience to purchase it directly from the women dressed in local costume who sit on stools outside their homes. Women dressed in black come into town as well in the mornings to sell their handicraft.

expensive but it's well worth the price. Pag lamb is also delicious, with the same wild herb taste.

Getting there

There is a bridge linking the south of the island to the mainland, and a ferry from Karlobag on the mainland to Pag Town. The Rijeka to Zadar bus passes through Novalja and Pag Town twice daily in each direction. For tourist information, the Novalja tourist office is at Šetalište hrvatskih mornara 1 ❶ 385 53 661 404 ⓦ www.tz-novalja.hr

SIGHTS & ATTRACTIONS

Beaches

The three main beaches are Straško, Zrče and Časka.

Pag Town

This is the administrative centre for the island and there's a mix of new and old. The town was actually established in the 15th century and has a medieval quality. The parish church of **Sv Marije** (St Mary's) is worth a visit, if only to see the rose window on the Gothic church facade that resembles the intricate pattern used in local lace. In Pag Town, there's a tiny **Lace Museum** just off the main square.

Novalja

This developed resort is about 20 km (12½ miles) north of Pag Town and lies close to several good beaches, so it attracts resort-seeking tourists and the all-night party crowd. **Zrče** beach, 2 km (1¼ miles) south of Novalja has become one of Croatia's hottest spots at night in the summer with clubs that stay open until dawn. The major

historical attraction nearby is the Roman town of Cissa or **Časka** (largely underwater) but there is an underground aqueduct with sections that you can visit. You enter through the **town museum**, whose collection includes amphorae from a 1st-century Roman ship.

AFTER DARK

Restaurants

Taverna Boskanic £–££ Looking down on Stara Novalja, this is where to meet locals over wine and raija and great platters of *pršut*, *paški sir* and sardines. ⓐ Stara Novalja

Natale ££ Right near the harbour in Pag Town, this restaurant specialises in Pag lamb and seafood – and also great *palačinke* and pizzas. ⓐ S. Radića 2 ⓣ 023 611 194

Restaurant Steffani ££ This is in the heart of Novalja and very popular with the locals as well as visitors. The usual seafood and lamb along with some local specialities like snails. ⓐ Petra Krešimira 1V 28

Hotel Restoran Biser ££–£££ This hotel restaurant has a terrace overlooking the sea and serves local fare, seafood and other Croatian specialities. ⓐ A.G. Matoša 7 ⓣ 023 611 333 ⓦ www.hotel-biser.com

Nightlife

The only nightclub is **Fifth Magazine**, which is based on the mainland side of the bridge in a warehouse that used to store salt. Novalja is where the action is and where young people head if they're looking for dancing, drinking, eating and socialising outdoors until the wee hours of the morning. There are a variety of clubs right on the beaches, so the party spills out onto the sand as DJs spin the latest in dance tracks. Each of the beaches has its following, but everyone's favourite, and the Novalja hotspot, is Zrče beach.

ACCOMMODATION

Biser ££ On a good beach in Pag Town, ensuite rooms (some with sea views), TV and air-conditioning. ⓐ A.G. Matoša 7 ⓣ 023 611 333 ⓦ www.hotel-biser.com

Pagus Hotel ££ On a small beach and central, the Pagus has spacious en-suite rooms. It was a 3-star but at the time of writing is being renovated up to a 4-star category. ⓐ Ante Starčevića 1 ⓣ 023 611 310 ⓔ hotel-pagus@coning.hr ⓦ www.coning.hr/hotelpagus

Hotel Plaza £££ The 4-star Plaza in Pag has smart en-suites plus other amenities such as a pool and fitness centre. ⓐ M. Marulica 14 ⓣ 023 600 855 ⓦ www.plaza-croatia.com

Valentino £££ Right in the heart of Pag Town, five luxury apartments with all the frills including kitchenettes, hydro-massage showers and internet availability. ⓐ A Danielli 2 ⓣ 023 600 800 ⓦ www.valentino-pag.com

For private accommodation, try the **Navalija Kompass** ⓐ Primorska ⓣ 023 661 215 ⓦ www.navalija-kompas.hr or **Maricom** ⓐ S Rodica 8 ⓣ 023 612 266

Plitvice Lakes National Park

While this stunning park is closer to Zagreb than it is to Dubrovnik, it is well worth a stop either on the way from the airport in Zagreb or on the way back. It's the country's oldest and largest national park and is on the UNESCO World Heritage list of sites – and little wonder. Sixteen emerald-green lakes spill one into the other via cataracts and waterfalls of varying height; the limestone rock around and in the lakes is a veritable artist's box of colours. The largest waterfall, **Veliki Slap**, is almost 70 m (230 ft) high. The water in the lakes hits every shade of green and blue and tree-shaded paths border the main lakes. The lakes are set in deep forests still populated by bears, wolves and wild boar, and cover nearly 300 sq km (116 sq miles).

GETTING THERE

Plitvice is about halfway between Zagreb and Zadar on the main road, with regular buses going from each of these and also from Split. There are two entry gates (Ulaz 1 in the north and Ulaz 2 in the south) each providing access to a different section of the lakes. Most of the park's infrastructure (hotels, tourist office, post office, restaurant) are closer to Ulaz 2. Getting back to Dubrovnik or Zagreb is a bit tricky since buses don't always stop, especially if they're full – you need to flag them down. ⓦ www.visit-croatia.co.uk/plitvicelakes

SIGHTS & ATTRACTIONS

Veliki Slap literally means 'the big waterfall', and big it is. This high wall of water is the park's main attraction and the dramatic focus of the lakes. Other highlights are the largest lake, Kozjak, and Labudovac Falls. The park is also rich in wildlife: alongside the bears and wolves live animals such as lynxes and otters, while birdwatchers can look out for rare species including the eagle, peregrine falcon, hoopoe, capercaillie and eagle owl. There are well-marked paths, walkways and bridges linking the main attractions; alternatively there are regular park buses and ferries for those who prefer a less strenuous day out.

⬤ *The breathtaking scenery of the Plitvice Lakes National Park*

TAKING A BREAK

Lička Kuća ££ This is a rustic mountain chalet type of place with wooden tables and chairs that serves traditional Lika food like roast lamb, spicy sausages and *đuveđ* (ratatouille flavoured with paprika). ❷ Opposite Ulaz 1 ❶ 385 53 751 024

ACCOMMODATION

Bellevue Hotel ££ Basic but not fancy hotel with 70 rooms (six singles), en-suite bathrooms. Popular with tour groups. ❷ Plitvička Jezera near Ulaz 2 ❶ 385 53 751 700. For more information ❶ 385 53 751 015

Hotel Jezero ££–£££ Built on high ground overlooking the lakes, this is definitely the most luxurious hotel in the park. Resembling a large mountain lodge, there are 210 rooms decorated in natural pinewood. There are tennis courts, a sauna, bowling alley and fitness centre. ❷ Plitvička Jezera ❶ 385 53 751 400

Private rooms These can be booked at the kiosks open in July and August and run by park authorities at both entry gates, Ulaz 1 and 2. At other times, the tourist office in the nearby village of Korenica (7 km/4¼ miles south of the lakes) will book private rooms ❶ 385 53 776 798. Also the tourist office in Rakovica (12 km/7 miles away) handles private room bookings. ❶ 385 47 784 450

▶ *Onofrio's Small Fountain, Dubrovnik*

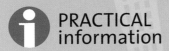

Directory

GETTING THERE
By air

The only year-round scheduled flights between the UK and Croatia are with Croatian Airways, which has daily flights from London Heathrow to Zagreb and once a week to Split. From May to October, Croatian Airways flies from Gatwick to Dubrovnik three times a week and Manchester to Dubrovnik twice a week. British Airways runs seasonal flights from London Gatwick to Split and Dubrovnik. The flights are not cheap although occasionally there are specials. The flights from London to Zagreb are just over two hours and about 30 minutes longer to Dubrovnik.

Anyone willing to do a little digging and research can find a considerably cheaper way to get to Dubrovnik by using one of the many budget airlines such as easyJet, Ryanair or Skyeurope; you can fly to a terminal in a nearby country and continue on by train or bus. easyJet, for example, has flights to Venice and Ljubljana, from where you can connect to Croatia by bus, ferry or rail. Another option is to use a hub city in Europe and then connect onto Zagreb or Dubrovnik: for example, Lufthansa flies to Zagreb from various UK airports via Frankfurt, and Malev has flights from London to Dubrovnik via Budapest.

Croatian Airlines ☏ 0 208 563 0022 ⓦ www.croatiaairlines.hr
British Airways ☏ 870 850 9850 ⓦ www.britishairways.com
easyJet ☏ 0870 600 0000 ⓦ www.easyjet.com
Ryanair ☏ 0870 156 9569l ⓦ www.ryanair.com

Many people are aware that air travel emits CO_2, which contributes to climate change. You may be interested in the possibility of lessening the environmental impact of your flight through the charity Climate Care, which offsets your CO_2 by funding environmental projects around the world. Visit www.climatecare.org

By rail

Travelling to Dubrovnik by rail is another option if you want to include other cities and travel in a leisurely way, but it's not an inexpensive choice. Rather than buy a return rail ticket to Croatia, it's wiser to invest in a rail pass and plan your own itinerary via an international rail timetable (see Ⓦ www.thomascookpublishing.com). There are a huge array of rail passes available, many of which must be bought before leaving home, while others can only be bought in the country for which they are valid. **Inter-Rail Passes** (available only for European residents) are available for 16 to 22 days or one month, and can be bought to cover two zones or all zones (global pass): 28 countries are grouped into zones. **Eurodomino Passes**, also only available to European residents, are individual country passes that provide unlimited travel in 25 European and North African countries. The pass allows you anything from three to eight days' extensive travel within a one-month period on the entire rail network of the chosen country.

A useful website for any kind of rail information: **The Man in Seat 61** Ⓦ www.seat61.com. **For Rail Europe** ❶ 0870 584 8848 Ⓦ www.raileurope.co.uk

By car

The most common road route from the UK to Dubrovnik is to take motorways from the Channel coast via Brussels, Cologne, Frankfurt, Munich, Salzburg and on to Ljubljana. From here take ordinary roads south to Rijeka on the Adriatic and then the coastal road through Split and on to Dubrovnik. Another route would be through France and Switzerland to Italy's Adriatic Coast and Bari, from where you can catch the ferry to Dubrovnik. The disadvantage of having a car is that parking in Dubrovnik is difficult and expensive: hotel car parks are full to overflowing and there is almost no street parking. The 'Sanitat Dubrovnik' mounts regular patrols to seek out illegally parked cars and will tow them away to a pound in Lapad.

By bus

If you're on a tight budget, the cheapest way to get to Croatia is by bus from the UK. **Eurolines** offers a return ticket daily from London to Zagreb that costs less than £200 and takes less than 34 hours to Zagreb and 38 to Split (two nights are spent on the road.) Eurolines also has a pass that links 46 European cities and will get you as far as Vienna – once there, you pay for an additional bus or train ticket to Zagreb or beyond. Eurolines ❶ 0870 514 3219 in the UK ⓦ www.eurolines.co.uk. Note: Going all the way by bus generally is longer and more expensive than taking a flight on a budget carrier to an Italian port and then the ferry across the Adriatic.

By ferry

There is ferry service to Croatia from several Italian Adriatic ports (Ancona, Bari, Civitanova and Pescara) run by four companies: Jadrolinija, SEM, SNAV and Adriatica Navigazione. If you're travelling by car, book well in advance especially in high season; if going on foot, you can usually buy tickets on arrival in Ancona or Bari. During peak travel times, there are also swift hydrofoil and catamaran services between Italian ports and Zadar and Split for passengers only. On overnight trips, you can pay less than £20 for a bed in a basic cabin. For timetables, contact the ferry companies:

Adriatica Navigazione ☎ 39 41 781 611 Ⓦ www.adriatica.it
Jadrolinija ☎ 385 51 666 111 Ⓦ www.jadrolinija.hr
SEM ☎ 385 21 338 292 Ⓦ www.sem-marina.hr
SNAV ☎ 39 71 207 6116 Ⓦ www.snav.it Ⓦ www.viamare.com

ENTRY FORMALITIES

Holders of full, valid EU, Canadian, US, Australian and New Zealand passports can enter Croatia without a visa for stays of up to 90 days (South Africans require a visa, obtainable in Pretoria). For longer stays, visa extensions are available by crossing the border into Italy or Slovenia and then re-entering. Other nationals require a visa for a small fee. Non EU nationals must provide evidence of sufficient funds (at least €100 per day). Theoretically, all visitors are required to register with the police but this is now a formality handled by the hotel clerks.

There is no duty on non-commercial goods brought in by visitors up to 30,000 Kn, although it is wise to register very expensive camera equipment or laptops. Also allowed: up to 200 cigarettes, one litre of spirits, two litres of wine, 500 g of coffee, 250 ml of perfume and up to 15,000 Kn in currency. For details on the rather complicated arrangements for reimbursement of VAT and other details: Ⓦ www.carina.hr

For further information on entry formalities check the Croatian Government website Ⓦ www.mvp.hr

MONEY

The main unit of currency is the kuna which is divided into 100 lipa. Coins come in denominations of 1, 5, 10 20 and 50 lipa and 1, 2 and 5 kuna. Notes (which depict Croatian heroes) come in denominations of 5, 19, 20, 50, 100, 500 and 1000 kuna. The currency gets its name from 'kuna', the Croatian word meaning 'marten' – in medieval days taxes were paid in pelts from the animal – and 'lipa', meaning linden tree. The euro is the secondary currency now, replacing the German mark, and the government tries to keep rates of exchange steady. The kuna is not a fully convertible currency, so you will need to buy it when you arrive and exchange it when you leave the country.

In main towns and cities, Automated Teller Machines (ATMs) are available to be used with internationally recognised cards. Check the symbol at the back of your card with those shown on the *bankomat*. Traveller's cheques can only be exchanged in a bank, and cash advances on American Express cards can be obtained from Atlas travel agency, wherever they have an office.

● *The kuna is the main unit of currency in Croatia*

Most commonly used credit cards (Visa, MasterCard, American Express, Diners and Sport Card International) are accepted in large shops, hotels, restaurants and resorts and can be used for cash advances in banks.

HEALTH, SAFETY & CRIME

Dubrovnik is a relatively safe destination with most food safe to eat and tap water safe to drink throughout the country. Croatians will tell you that they have the cleanest water in Europe and, looking at the crystal-clear lakes and rivers, you're inclined to believe them. No inoculations are required for travel to Croatia, but anyone planning to do some trekking in the mountains should investigate being inoculated against tick-borne encephalitis. (Spray generously with tick repellents and wear long trousers tucked into your boots and a hat.)

There is a reciprocal agreement between Croatia and the EU countries for free health care, but sometimes certain services are not available in the public hospitals and you will have to be treated privately. Since private care is not cheap, it's a wise idea to take out health insurance for major emergencies. Small medical problems are usually treated at one of Dubrovnik's pharmacies (*ljekarna*), where there is usually someone who speaks English. Pharmacies are usually open 08.00–19.00 Mon–Fri & 08.00–14.00 Sat. They operate a rota system, so there's usually one pharmacy open at night-time and on weekends (check the posting on the window of the pharmacy).

For more serious problems, head for the nearest hospital (*bolnica* or *klilnicki centar*). Normal hospital treatment is free to citizens of most EU countries on producing a valid passport. Hospitals are clean and well run, although there might be a shortage

of Western drugs. The most common complaints seem to be sunburn, seasickness, insect bites and stepping on sea urchin spikes.

Croatia is relatively safe when it comes to crime, but petty theft can occur and the best defence here is common sense. Don't flash around a lot of money, don't carry a wallet in a hip pocket and don't wear expensive jewellery. It's a good idea to take out travel insurance before you leave and take photocopies of all your documents, credit cards, etc. Streets should be reasonably safe at night, but single women should remember this is a patriarchal society and a woman alone can find herself the target of Mediterranean male machismo.

OPENING HOURS

The usual opening hours for shops is 07.00–20.00 Monday to Friday and 08.00–14.00 or 15.00 on Saturday. Food stores such as the supermarkets will generally stay open until 18.00 on Saturday and will open on Sunday mornings as well. Open-air markets are normally open from 07.00–13.00 Monday to Saturday and from 07.00–11.00 on Sunday. Clothing shops and bookshops are open from 09.00–13.00 and from 17.00–19.30 Monday to Friday; also from 09.00–13.00 on Saturday. These hours may vary in the summer months in tourist centres particularly. Banks are generally open from 08.00–17.00 from Monday to Friday and from 08.00–11.00 or 12.00 noon on Saturday. Usual hours at post offices are 07.00–19.00 Monday to Friday and 08.00–13.00 or 14.00 on Saturday.

TOILETS

Every restaurant and bar will have a toilet, but it's a good idea to cough up for an espresso or drink if you do use their facilities. Public toilets (*zahod* or WC) in town are more difficult to find, but those that do exist are usually clean, well-stocked and hygienic. In trains and bus stations, the public facilities usually come with a small charge of a couple of kn. Men use facilities marked *Muški* and women's are *Ženski*.

CHILDREN

Croats love children – their own and those of visitors as well. Children tend to stay up late and, instead of being left with a babysitter, will often accompany their parents to a late dinner in a restaurant. Croatian pizzas tend to be close to the originals from Naples and popular with kids. Try Mea Culpa ❷ Za Rokom 3 where the pizzas are inexpensive and tables outside so that kids don't have to be shushed. Ice-cream parlours are also popular with children; the best is Dolce Vita on Nalješkovićeva.

The Adriatic waters are clear and fantastic for swimming, but be warned that many beaches are pebbly rather than sandy and there may be sea urchins about, so take jelly beach shoes for non-swimmers or younger children.

Cycles are widely available for hire, particularly in the national and nature parks, and children will enjoy exploring the flatter islands such as Mljet on two wheels. Bikes, kayaks and other vehicles can be hired at Mali Most near Mali Jezerto or the Hotel Odisej for around 30 kn an hour. Boat trips are another effortless way of entertaining children. Most organised trips include lunch and a chance to swim. A trip in a glass-bottomed cruise boat is an ideal way of introducing children to the marine life of the area. Check out Marko Polo in Korčula Town and Ⓦ www.korculainfo.com

Festivals always provide fun for the family, particularly those that are dedicated to younger audiences, such as the Puppet Theatre Festival in Osijek (early May). Children will also enjoy the Moreška

dance, performed through the summer in Korcula, which is a dramatic dance using real swords.

For visitors on longer stays there are wonderful kids' camps that offer highly creative arts programmes, sailing, language lessons and a lot more. See ⓦ www.adriatica.net/kids

COMMUNICATIONS

Communications are smooth and trouble-free generally with reasonable prices. Internet cafes are common in all Croatian cities and are relatively cheap, except you may be required to register, so have a passport handy.

Internet access

Using the internet is popular, so there are special internet cafés, tourist agency rooms with computers, or sometimes just a lonely computer in the corner of a bar (cost is usually around 20 to 30 Kn per hour). Top-end hotels have ISDN lines in the rooms but dial-up connections can be slow. Some of the internet places use a Croatian keyboard, so ask for help – web addresses omit the accents. In Dubrovnik, try The Internet Centar, Ante Starčivićev ⓔ 7, Pile; Internet Prijeko 15, close to Don Corleone Pizza; and Holobit, Šetalište kralja Zvonimira 56 in Lapad.

Telephones

Public phones use magnetic cards called *telekarta* and these can be purchased at newspaper kiosks or from the post office. Rates change according to the time you call with peak times from 07.00–22.00; Sunday has a 50 per cent discount. For local directory enquiries call 988; international directory enquiries 902 and for weather or road conditions 902.

Mobile phones from North America encounter problems in Europe, so an international mobile phone like the **Mobal World Phone** is highly recommended. This is advertised as the cheapest way to use mobile phones abroad and it works in 140 countries once it's set up. There are no minimums, service charges or fees – you pay only for the calls you make. Unlike other SIM card systems, with the Mobal World Phone the calls you make are debited from your credit card. Each user has a lifetime phone number that can be reached in any of the 140 countries.

Post office

Stamps (called *marka* or plural *marke*) can be bought at the posta – look for a sign of a yellow spiral with a triangle on the end. You can also buy stamps from newsagents and tobacco kiosks. Post boxes are canary yellow. Stamps for postcards sent to a destination in the EU cost 4Kn (takes around five days); postcards to North America cost 5Kn and take about two weeks. Letters are priced according to weight and parcels should be left open for inspection by the post office before you send them.

Telephoning abroad

For the best rates, go to phone booths in post offices or kiosks rather than the hotel. Dial 00 and then the country code (UK 44; USA and Canada 1; Australia 61; New Zealand 64), then dial the number, omitting the first zero of the area code.

ELECTRICITY

Croatia uses 220 volts and round, two-pin plugs. If you need an adaptor, get one before you leave home.

PRACTICAL INFORMATION

TRAVELLERS WITH DISABILITIES

It was ironically the 1991–2 war that raised the profile of disabled travellers because of the large number of wounded and physically disabled people that the war created. In larger towns and cities, many public places, such as railway stations and airports, are wheelchair accessible, and there are a growing number of hotels that take wheelchairs into consideration. Tourism offices will generally check accommodation for facilities for a visitor, but it's wise to double check with the hotel itself.

Additional information in English is published in a guide by Savez Organizacija Invalida Hrvatske (ⓐ Savska Cesta 3 10000 Zagreb ❶ 385 01 482 9394 ✉ soih@zg.htnet.hr ⓦ www.soih.hr). Holiday Care (❶ 0845 1249971 ⓦ www.holidaycare.org.uk) has basic information on facilities for disabled people in various countries.

▲ *Bus routes are clearly marked*

FURTHER INFORMATION

The main **tourist information office** in Dubrovnik will hand out maps and brochures as well as making bookings for concerts and other events. To reach this office, go through the Pile Gate and walk about 200 m up the hill to ⓐ Ante Starčićeva 7 ⓣ 020 323 887 ⓔ info@tzdubrovnik.hr ⓦ www.tzdubrovnik.hr. There are two smaller tourism offices, one at Miha Pracata and the other next door to the Jadrolinija ticket office in Gruž.

To read up further on your destination before leaving for Dubrovnik, you can contact the Croatian National Tourist Office ⓐ 2 The Lanchesters, 162–164 Fulham Palace Rd, London W69ER ⓣ 020 085 637 979 ⓕ 563 2616 ⓦ www.croatia.hr. Staff there will provide answers to questions plus supply lots of brochures, information about accommodation and maps of specific towns and resorts.

In Croatia, all towns and regions have tourist information centres and, while they can offer names and addresses for accommodation, many don't book on your behalf.

Websites

Most towns and resorts will have a website that you can look up and most have an English version.

ⓦ **www.croatia.hr** is the official website for the Croatian National Tourist Board and this offers a large amount of information from history to accommodation and dining to links to other sites.

ⓦ **www.tzdubrovnik.hr** is the best of the sites covering Dubrovnik and the surrounding area.

ⓦ **www.adriatica.net** has general information about Adriatic resorts with an online booking service handling apartments, villas and hotels.

...ul phrases

...ough English is widely spoken in Croatia, these words and ...rases may come in handy. See also the phrases for specific situations in other parts of the book.

English	Croatian	Approx. pronunciation
BASICS		
Yes	Da	Da
No	Ne	Ne
Please	Molim	Mo-lim
Thank you	Hvala	Hva-la
Hello	Zdravo	Zdra-vo
Goodbye	Zbogom	Zbo-gom
Excuse me	Oprostite	O-`pro-sti-te
Sorry	Pardon	Par-don
That's O.K.	To je u redu	To ye oo re-doo
To	U	Oo
From	Iz	Iz
I don't speak Croatian	(Ja) ne govorim hrvatski	(Ja) ne `go-vo-rim `hr-vat-ski
Do you speak English?	Govorite li engleski?	`Go-vo-ri-te li `en-gle-ski
Good morning	Dobro jutro	Do-bro yoo-tro
Good afternoon	Dobar dan	Do-bar dan
Good evening	Dobra veĕer	Do-bra ve-cher
Good night	Laku noć	La-koo noch
My name is ...	Moje ime je ...	Mo-ye ime ye ...
DAYS & TIMES		
Monday	Ponedjeljak	Po-`ne-die-llak
Tuesday	Utorak	`Oo-to-rak
Wednesday	Srijeda	Srie-da
Thursday	Četvrtak	Che-`tvr-tak
Friday	Petak	Pe-tak
Saturday	Subota	`Soo-bo-ta
Sunday	Nedjelja	`Ne-die-lla
Morning	Jutro	Yoo-tro
Afternoon	Popodne	Po-`po-dne
Evening	Veĕer	Ve-cher
Night	Noć	Noty
Yesterday	Juĕer	Yoo-cher

English	Croatian	Approx. pronunciation
Today	Danas	Da-nas
Tomorrow	Sutra	Soo-tra
What time is it?	Koliko je sati?	`Ko-li-ko ye sa-ti
It is ...	Točno ...	Toch-no ...
09.00	Devet sati	De-vet sa-ti
Midday	Podne	Pod-ne
Midnight	Ponoć	Po-noch

NUMBERS

One	Jedan	Ye-dan
Two	Dva	Dva
Three	Tri	Tri
Four	Četri	`Che-ti-ri
Five	Pet	Pet
Six	Šest	Shest
Seven	Sedam	Se-dam
Eight	Osam	O-sam
Nine	Devet	De-vet
Ten	Deset	De-set
Eleven	Jedanaest	Ye-`da-na-est
Twelve	Dvanaest	`Dva-na-est
Twenty	Dvadeset	`Dva-de-set
Fifty	Pedeset	Pe-`de-set
One hundred	Sto	Sto

MONEY

I would like to change these travellers' cheques/this currency	Želio bih unovčiti ove putničke čekove. Želio bih promijeniti ovaj novac	`Zhe-li-o bih oo-`nov-chi-ti ove `poot-nich-ke `che-ko-ve. `zhe-li-o bih pro-`mie-ni-ti o-vay no-vac
Where is the nearest ATM?	Gdje je najbliži bankomat?	Gdye ye nay-bli-zhi ban-ko-mat?
Do you accept traveller's cheques/credit cards?	Mogu li platiti putničkim čekovima/ kreditnom karticom?	Mo-goo li `pla-ti-ti `poot-nich-kim `che-ko-vi-ma/ kre-dit-nom `kar-ti-tsom?

SIGNS & NOTICES

Airport	Aerodrom	`A-e-ro-drom
Entrance	Ulaz	Oo-laz
Exit	Izlaz	Iz-laz
Smoking/ non-smoking	Za pušače/za nepušače (Zabranjeno pušenje)	Za poo-`sha-che/za `ne-poo-sha-che (za-bra-nye-no `poo-she-nye)
Toilets	WC	Ve tse
Ladies/Gentlemen	Muški/Ženski	Moosh-ki/Zhen-ski

Emergencies

EMERGENCY NUMBERS

The three numbers to memorise are: 94 for an ambulance, 92 for the police and 93 for fire. The public emergency centre is on 985.

HOSPITAL
Roka Misetica

In Lapad, 4 km (2½ miles) west of Old Town, 24-hour service.
☎ 020 431 777

Pharmacies

There are a dozen or more pharmacies (called *ljekarne* here) in Dubrovnik, with three on Stradun. **⏱** 08.00–20.00 Mon–Fri & 08.00–14.00 Sat. Two pharmacies take turns to be open 24 hours a day: **Kod Zvonika** **ⓐ** Stradun **☎** 020 321 133 and **Ljekarna Gruz** **ⓐ** Gruzka obala, just up from Hotel Petka **☎** 020 418 990

CONSULATES & EMBASSIES

While most of the consulates are headquartered in Zagreb, there are a few offices in Dubrovnik: the Austrian Consulate, the Royal Danish Consulate and the Consulate of the United Kingdom of Great Britain and Northern Ireland, **ⓐ** A Bunićeva Poljana 3/I **☎** 020 324 597. There are honorary consulates for the Netherlands and Spain.

BACKGROUND READING

Balkan Ghosts by Robert Kaplan. As a political look at the tortured politics in the area, Kaplan bases his insightful comments on an extensive trip in 1990. A good read.

Black Lamb and Grey Falcon by Rebecca West. This is one of the classic travel books for the area and it has both fans and detractors. The first quarter of the book is about Croatia.

Café Europa by Slavenka Drakulic. One of Croatia's leading novelists, Drakulic's collection of essays has a section on Croatia and the flowering of nationalism.

Croatia: a Nation Forged in War by Marcus Tanner. An enthusiastic, balanced and totally thorough look at the general history of Croatia, written by a journalist who witnessed the country's break-up.

Explaining Yugoslavia by John B. Allcock. For anyone curious about how such a disparate bunch of nations were pasted together to form Yugoslavia, this is a knowledgeable and stimulating historical account.

Through the Embers of Chaos by Dervla Murphy. A look at the countries of former Yugoslavia by a well-known travel writer.

The publishers would like to thank the following for supplying the copyright photos for this book: page 7 Andrija Carlli/Croatian National Tourist Board; pages 16, 23, 25, 30, 68, 108, 152 Jon Smith; page 19 Toomas Jarvet; page 35 Irida Banac/Croatian National Tourist Board; pages 39, 40, 103, 146 Croatian National Tourist Board; pages 61, 97 Darko Barisic; page 65 Ivo Pervan/Croatian National Tourist Board; pages 75, 141 Pictures Colour Library; page 130 Juraj Kopac/Croatian National Tourist Board; page 133 Romeo Ibrisevic/Croatian National Tourist Board; all the rest Helena Zukowski.

Copy editor: Penny Isaac
Proofreader: Natasha Reed

Send your thoughts to
books@thomascook.com

- Found a great bar, club, shop or must-see sight that we don't feature?
- Like to tip us off about any information that needs updating?
- Want to tell us what you love about this handy little guidebook and more importantly how we can make it even handier?

Then here's your chance to tell all! Send us ideas, discoveries and recommendations today and then look out for your valuable input in the next edition of this title. As an extra 'thank you' from Thomas Cook Publishing, you'll be automatically entered into our exciting monthly prize draw.

Send an email to the above address (stating the book's title) or write to: CitySpots Project Editor, Thomas Cook Publishing, PO Box 227, The Thomas Cook Business Park, Unit 18, Coningsby Road, Peterborough PE3 8SB, UK.